THE
NEW RIGHT
HUMANITARIANS

Tom Barry . **Deb Preusch** . **Beth Sims**
THE RESOURCE CENTER . $5.00

First Printing 1986
Second Printing 1986

ISBN: 0-911213-07-4

Tom Barry and Deb Preusch are co-directors of the Resource Center and Beth Sims is a member of the staff. Beth Wood edited the manuscript. The Resource Center is grateful for comments on the manuscript from Russ Bellant, Karen Branan, and Joy Hackel. Judith Kidd designed the cover and Jack Kutz designed the charts. Jerre Jenkins and Sally Gwylan assisted with word processing.

Table of Contents

Tables, Graphs, and Diagrams

Introduction

Over the last few years private financial and material support has helped the contras weather dry spells in the flow of U.S. government aid and has greatly assisted pacification programs in El Salvador and Guatemala. Among certain sectors, the support has been enthusiastic. An array of organizations and powerful individuals have enlisted in the anticommunist crusade.

Responding to President Reagan's call for more private support to Central America, General Harry Aderholt, head of the Air Commandos Association, said, "Maybe we in the private sector can take over and win down there." Tom Reisinger, the director of Refugee Relief International, also declared his organization's willingness to join the effort: "We believe in President Reagan's challenge for the private sector to parallel government efforts in supplying needed assistance to those suffering in the midst of armed conflicts."

This Resource Center report examines the origins and the operations of the circle of private organizations involved in this effort. And it focuses on the following ways that these organizations support the Reagan administration's policies in Central America:

* Formulating a popular ideology of counterrevolution.

* Building public support for the contras.

* Providing non-lethal aid for pacification programs.

* Serving as a front for CIA operations.

* Supplying mercenaries and military equipment and training.

* Lobbying for more aid to the contras and other counterrevolutionary forces.

Part One of the report, The New Right Network, describes the rise of New Right and outlines its ideology. It provides short biographies of key personalities and examines how a network of think tanks and political pressure groups form the institutional backbone of the right wing. This section also shows how the anticommunist ideology of the New Right and the related U.S. military doctrine on low intensity conflict provide a structure for U.S. private support for counterrevolutionary forces in the region.

Part Two, The Central America Connection, looks at how the New Right and allied organizations actively support counterrevolution in the region. This network has been tapped by the Reagan administration to provide financial support and public backing for U.S. economic and military intervention in Central America. Most of the groups involved assert that their primary goal is to distribute "humanitarian assistance" to refugees and other victims of violence in Central America. This section reveals the deceptive nature of that claim and shows instead that the objective of these "humanitarian" aid programs is to further counterrevolution. Most of this private aid flows to the very areas where the contras have their bases, providing critical economic support for the rebels and their families.

Also examined in Part Two are the close links among private groups and the military and intelligence agencies. Rather than an independent expression of U.S. political sentiment, the private supply lines to Central America are closely coordinated with the U.S. government's own counterinsurgency apparatus in the region. So prevalent and dominant is government influence that the assistance distributed in Central America can hardly qualify as "private."

Parts Three and Four feature an annotated listing of the think tanks, lobbying organizations, and public pressure groups of the New Right network followed by a listing of groups providing financial support for counter revolution in Central America—either in the form of military assistance or non-lethal aid. These sections reveal the close links between all these groups and their connections with the U.S. government.

SUMMARY OF FINDINGS

The following is a summary of the major findings of this report:

* The phenomenon of private groups aiding counterinsurgency and counterrevolutionary campaigns supported by the U.S. government is not a new one. Many of the leading figures and organizations currently involved in Central America played a similar role during the Vietnam war.

* A close knit network of right-wing organizations provides the main private support for the Reagan administration's program of counterrevolution in Central America.

* Private organizations are an important source of aid not only for the contras but also for pacification and civic action programs in El Salvador and Guatemala.

* A cornerstone for the private campaign is the military doctrine of low intensity conflict that advocates the increased use of humanitarian assistance in third world conflicts and support of surrogate counterrevolutionary forces.

* The private counterrevolutionary campaign is an integral part of covert war and psychological operations in the region.

* The many private organizations supporting counterrevolution in Central America are not working separately but are part of a network coordinated by retired U.S. generals and government officials.

* Prominent in this network are many military and CIA figures who have specialized in unconventional warfare, covert operations, and military civic action programs.

* Also included in the private network are numerous individuals with racist and neo-Nazi connections.

* The fundraising campaign for Nicaraguan refugees serves as an effective anti-Sandinista propaganda device.

* Many private organizations function as front groups for the CIA and hardline anticommunist groups.

* This campaign also has given a cloak of legitimacy to a number of extreme anticommunist groups formerly ignored by the public and the media.

* Much of the money raised by these groups never gets to Central America but is used for propaganda purposes here in the United States.

* The Reagan administration has encouraged the politicization of private voluntary organizations and many now serve as instruments of U.S. policy.

* The politicized nature of these groups blurs the distinction between all private and U.S. government operations in the region.

* Likewise, the involvement of the Pentagon, CIA, and National Security Council in "humanitarian assistance" further blurs the distinction between U.S. military and economic assistance programs in Central America.

* The so-called "humanitarian assistance" and "non-lethal aid" being distributed has contributed to continued terrorism and military repression in Central America.

* The campaign to aid the contras has created a dangerous coalition of hardline anticommunists, militarists, mercenaries, and New Right leaders that operate in tandem with officials from the Pentagon, CIA, and National Security Council. This coalition currently focuses on support for Nicaraguan contras, but this web of connections could be tapped for other foreign or possibly domestic ventures.

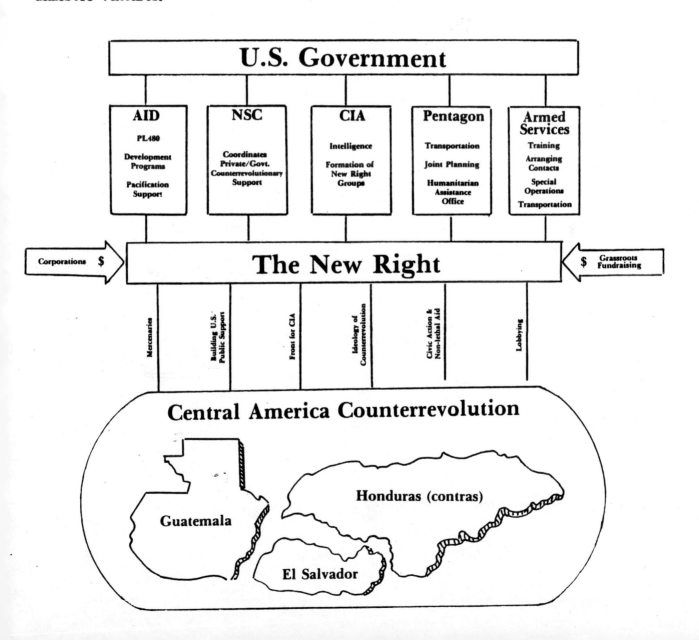

Part One

The New Right Network

At first glance, the private groups providing support for the contras and the Guatemalan and Salvadoran armies appear to be an unlikely mish-mash of groups and individuals with widely varying goals and backgrounds. Those involved range from housewives collecting toys for refugee children to Texas oilmen buying airplanes and anti-aircraft guns for the contra army. Television evangelists, Moonies, and elite Catholics all play a part. The movement brings in university intellectuals, uneducated true believers, soldiers of fortune, white supremacists, retired generals, and high government officials. You can participate by attending $500-a-plate dinners or by donating disposable razors to the contras.

But it's not all so haphazard and unpredictable as it sounds. The disparate elements are brought together by a small, intricate network of financiers, ideologues, and activists. Its origins can be traced back to the McCarthy era of the 1950s when Cold War anticommunism was sweeping through the country. However it was not until the 1964 presidential campaign of Barry Goldwater that the outlines of the New Right began to truly take shape. Goldwater's statement, "Extremism in the defense of liberty is no vice," was their early rallying cry.

In the wake of Goldwater's unsuccessful campaign, the New Rightists broke with the traditional conservatives and set out to form their own institutions and build their own constituency. While traditional conservatives came from a narrow bourgeois sector of proprietors and intellectuals, the New Right looked for their support among middle America. Unlike the traditional conservatives, the New Right was not as concerned with respectability and has not shied away from incorporating fringe elements like white supremacists, TV preachers, and rabid anticommunists into their midst. And the New Right tapped into widespread dissatisfaction with big government, big labor, and what was seen as the general drift away from basic values of God, family, and country. It vowed to "Make America Great Again."

The crisis in the Nixon administration and the Watergate scandal of 1974 left the Republican party in shambles, and New Rightists like Ronald Reagan were eager to pick up the pieces and restructure the party in their own image. They did not win the party's presidential nomination in 1976 but during the Carter administration they began to push forward showing their ever-increasing strength. They dismissed Carter's human rights policies and his administration's commitment to negotiated settlements of third world crises as accommodation to the Soviets. The New Right demanded that Uncle Sam flex his muscles and shake off the so-called Vietnam syndrome of non-intervention.

By the time Ronald Reagan announced his candidacy in 1980, the New Right network had become a powerful movement that offered him widespread public support and an extreme political agenda. This network not only has supplied the administration with the ideological and strategic framework for its policies in Central America, but the network has also offered critical material support for the forces of counterrevolution in the region.

New Right Populism

Paul Weyrich, commonly regarded as the New Right's main tactician, says that little difference exists between the old-line and the New Right conservatives—it's mainly a question of tactics and self-image. Whereas the traditional conservatives are a "phenomenon of the upper classes" and characterized by a "highly intellectual strain," the New Right has eschewed the scholarly approach and framed its politics in the language of the middle class and blue-collar workers. Whereas the old right has had a pessimistic view of its political future, Weyrich says the New Right "believes it can win." Fired up by religion and anticommunist paranoia, New Rightists are righteous and determined. "A common assumption of New Right activists is that government should support certain moral truths."[1]

In the 1970s, the New Right was busy creating a strategy for winning. The New Right stressed the importance of mass organizing, sloganeering, press conferences, media manipulation, and public relations. Weyrich explains the new approach: "The Old Right did not understand anything at all about mass psychology, since they came from a different, pre-television era. [The Old Right] never did much to try to persuade them to be dramatic, to think big. The New Right recognizes that technology, like the media, is morally neutral and exists to be taken advantage of by anybody."[2]

In many ways, then, the difference between the New Right and traditional conservatives is more a matter of style and appearances than substance. Both factions oppose social services, promote unfettered capitalism, and back increased military spending.

Members of the Club

The institutional base of the New Right is a web of think tanks, lobbying organizations, and public pressure groups. This network is characterized by its interlocking directorships and its assumed role as the defender of democracy, family, and Christian values. Above all, however, anticommunism is the glue that holds the network together.

Right-wing think tanks have generated ideological justifications, scholarly analyses, and policy alternatives which have been adopted both by the administration and by the leadership of the New Right. In addition, they have served as recruitment pools for the current administration. Several older, traditionally conservative think tanks like the Hoover Institution on War, Revolution, and Peace (established in 1919, Ronald Reagan is an honorary fellow) serve the flourishing right-wing movement. The American Enterprise Institute, founded in 1943, and the Center for Strategic and International Studies, founded in 1962, also have a traditional conservative base and have provided the New Right with key leaders and policy positions.

The Heritage Foundation, formed in 1974, is the New Right's leading think tank. In defense related issues, the National Strategy Information Center is a major source of New Right policies.

Joining New Right think tanks are lobbying, political action, and public pressure groups that publicize their agenda to the electorate and lobby for their programs in Washington. Some of these are older groups that have been revived or reenergized by the New Right movement and the Reagan administration while others are direct offsprings of the New Right. Organizations like the American Security Council and the Coalition for Peace through Strength are mainly military lobbies. Then there are groups like The Conservative Caucus that concentrate on lobbying in Washington for the entire conservative New Right agenda.

Other organizations like the Liberty Federation and the Eagle Forum organize public pressure for their political programs. These groups perform the vital function of popularizing the New Right's ideology. In collaboration with the CIA, they sponsor press conferences and speaking tours of contra leaders and such extreme right-wing figures as Roberto D'Aubuisson.

The evangelists, who bring their message of God, country, and anticommunism to the masses, have proved to be a crucial part of the New Right formula for success. Media ministers like Jimmy Swaggart, Pat Robertson, and Jerry Falwell have integrated New Right politics into their sermons. The religious rightists have provided the New Right with the popular base and financial support essential to its success.

Working along parallel lines with the New Right is another set of institutions associated with the neoconservatives. These are academics, right-wing Democrats, professionals, journalists, and labor leaders who, while sharing many of the values of the New Right, are uncomfortable with its anti-intellectualism and uncompromising postures. Neoconservative institutions include the Committee for the Free World and the Institute for Religion and Democracy.

The shared values of the New Right network permit a division of labor according to expertise and spheres of influence: business elites generate cash; ideologues push policy; religious leaders and direct mail specialists stir up popular support. With the private sector mobilized, politicians and the military attend to legislation, coordination, and implementation of the New Right's program.

New Right Profiles

A small group of key individuals fill the letterheads of the New Right organizations. People like Paul Weyrich, Richard Viguerie, and Howard Phillips are familiar names in the small circle of New Right leadership. Behind these men and their organizations are the moneybags like Joseph Coors, Richard Mellon Scaife, Nelson Bunker Hunt, and Patrick Frawley. The main philanthropic foundations that prop up the New Right include the J. Howard Pew Freedom Trust, Sarah Scaife Foundation, Smith Richardson Foundation, and the Lilly Foundation.[3] The following are profiles of several selected New Right figures:

L. Francis Bouchey: Bouchey was the former Washington representative of the American-Chilean Council which lobbied for the Pinochet military regime. He is the executive vice-president of the Council for Inter-American Security and co-authored the influential Santa Fe Document. Bouchey has organized and chaired many CAUSA seminars.

Joseph Coors: See Profile in Part II.

Jeremiah Denton: The U.S. senator from Alabama is a Senate co-chair of the Coalition for Peace through Strength. The Conservative Digest has consistently named him as one of the ten most admired conservative members of Congress; and the National Journal in 1983 rated him as the most conservative senator. The American Security Council gave Denton a 100 percent voting index rating in 1984. He has served as a consultant to the Christian Broadcasting Network, founded the Coalition for Decency, and is a member of the Knights of Malta. At the urging of Andy Messing of the National Defense Council, he sponsored and obtained approval for the 1985 Denton Amendment which allows the U.S. military to transport private humanitarian relief supplies to Central America.

Roger Fontaine: The son-in-law of Ray Cline, former CIA deputy director, Fontaine recently served as the Latin American spe-

cialist on Reagan's National Security Council. Before joining the Reagan administration, Fontaine was the director of Latin American studies at the Center for Strategic and International Studies. As an associate of the Council for Inter-American Security, Fontaine co-authored the organization's influential Santa Fe Document. Recently he has worked as a reporter for the Washington Times, and he participated in the annual World Anti-Communist League meeting in 1985.

Patrick Frawley: Once called "the wealthiest man on the far right," Frawley was born in Nicaragua, where his father was a successful investor. An active supporter of the American Security Council, Frawley, who was a main backer of Ronald Reagan's campaign for governor, launched the Paper-Mate company which later bought out the Eversharp, Schick, and Technicolor companies. He supports the following groups: American Security Council, Young Americans for Freedom, Moral Re-Armament, Council of the Americas, Hoover Institution, Freedoms Foundation, and Up with People. Frawley-controlled companies own several right-wing Catholic publications, including the National Catholic Register, that support counterrevolution in Central America. Fred Schlafly, a director of the World Anti-Communist League and husband of Phyllis Schlafly, has worked for the Frawley business consortium.

Howard Phillips: The head of the powerful Conservative Caucus, Phillips is considered a brilliant grassroots organizer. He rose to prominence when President Nixon appointed him to dismantle the Office of Economic Opportunity. Phillips, who favors "a return to Biblical law," was a member of the New Right coalition headed by James Whelan of the Washington Times that monitored the National Bipartisan Commission on Central America. He co-founded the Moral Majority, and together with Paul Weyrich helped get "electronic ministers" like Falwell and Robertson into politics. Phillips is a leading supporter of the World Anti-Communist League and has sponsored John Birch Society tours to South Africa to meet government and military leaders.

Richard Mellon Scaife: Great-grandson of the founder of the Mellon empire (Gulf Oil), Scaife funds most major conservative institutions, particularly those involved in the formation of public opinion. His philanthropic work is handled by the Sarah Scaife, Allegheny and Carthage Foundations. Since it began operating 12 years ago, Scaife has given over $4 million to the Heritage Foundation. He also supports the Center for Strategic and International Studies, National Strategy Information Center, Committee on the Present Danger, Institute for Foreign Policy Analysis, Committee for a Free World, Hoover Institution, Accuracy in Media, American Legislative Exchange Council, and Free Congress Foundation. Each year Scaife gives about $10 million to right-wing groups.

William E. Simon: Simon, who was treasury secretary during the Nixon administration, has been described as a "free enterprise warrior." In his book A Time for Truth, Simon calls on the business community to create a Republican/conservative "counter-intelligensia" and advocates that "multi-millions" be given to foundations that are "imbued with the philosophy of freedom." He proposed that "non-egalitarian scholars" be given grants to produce the information and analysis needed to educate America. Simon is a former or current associate of the American Enterprise Institute, Accuracy in Media, and the Heritage Foundation. He is also a leading figure in Americares, Knights of Malta, and the Nicaraguan Freedom Fund.

Richard Viguerie: Viguerie is a direct mail specialist who operates out of Falls Church, Virginia. His direct mail and information empire offers public relations services to New Right causes. Until recently the publisher of the Conservative Digest, Viguerie was also a participant in a coalition that monitored the Kissinger Commission.

Paul Weyrich: A former press secretary and broadcast journalist, Weyrich has used those skills to organize the New Right. He and Joseph Coors founded the Free Congress Foundation and the Heritage Foundation. He conceived the name Moral Majority and co-founded the organization with Jerry Falwell and Howard Phillips. "We are radicals working to overturn the present power structures in this country," says Weyrich, who stresses the importance of organizing the middle and working classes around religious and social issues rather than economic and fiscal ones. Weyrich also serves as treasurer of the Council on National Policy.

New Right Ideology and Strategy

Traditional conservatism before World War II was an isolationist brand of politics. After the war, however, the right wing embraced the hysteria of Cold War anticommunism, giving their unqualified support to the containment and counterinsurgency politics of the Truman, Eisenhower, and Kennedy administrations. The conservatives of the 1960s felt that both political parties were becoming too accommodating with the red menace. They called for a more active defense of the "free world."

The anticommunism of the New Right is an uncompromising ideology that says there can be no accommodation between East and West. They call for reduced development aid and for the increased use of such instruments of low intensity conflict as special operations, psychological operations, and military civic action.

In their hard-line view of the Soviet Union, New Right leaders see a "hungry bear" with an appetite gone wild, gorging itself first on Eastern Europe, but inevitably turning its ravenous eye toward the rest of the globe, with Central America being the current target. For the New Right, the world is divided in two: ours and theirs. "Theirs" is ever-expanding; "ours" is ever-threatened. Thus, in any conflict—even those with acknowledged indigenous roots—the Soviets are seen to be the hidden enemy. This bi-polar view of the world conveniently overlooks such phenomena as the Sino-Soviet split, the rise of the Non-Aligned Movement, and the proliferation of internally based third world struggles.

What is distinctive about the New Right's anticommunism is not its polarized view of world politics but its fight-back strategy. Instead of simply taking measures to contain the growth of leftist states, New Right ideologues support military measures to roll back the advances of world communism. Born in the New Right think tanks, this policy has become known as the Reagan Doctrine.

In Central America, the Reagan Doctrine promotes fighting the Soviets on what is considered their own terms, with their own weapons: armed revolutionaries, psychological operations, destabilization, and strategic alliances. Robert Moffit of the Council for Inter-American Security (CIS) says this strategy is based in the "new international politics of reciprocity"—a tit-for-tat policy that calls for the United States to react point by point to perceived acts of Soviet aggression.[4] In this view, if the Soviets support leftist revolutionary movements in the third world, the United States should similarly arm and support rightist movements.

This roll back strategy was a prominent part of the Heritage Foundation's set of policy prescriptions for Reagan's second term. The foundation's Mandate II recommended the underwriting of paramilitary forces—renamed "freedom fighters"—in nine countries that "threaten United States' interests." The authors argued that such a policy would show that the U.S. "no longer will countenance the subversion or overthrow of friendly governments within the developing world."[5]

In the Central American context, the Reagan Doctrine is supported by a document that has historical and ideological significance for the region. The Monroe Doctrine was promulgated in 1823 by President James Monroe to announce a "hands off" policy for the Western Hemisphere. Monroe declared to the European powers, which had obvious colonial intentions, the newly independent nations of the Americas were to be left alone. Significantly, Monroe's doctrine neglected to include the United States in the restriction. As a consequence, the doctrine has often been invoked to justify U.S. intervention in the internal affairs of Latin American nations.

Recently, the Monroe Doctrine has been dredged up again to defend U.S. activities in Central America.   The Conservative Caucus (TCC), a right-wing grassroots lobby which has sent humanitarian aid to the Nicaraguan contras, recommended the revitalization of the Monroe Doctrine in one of its information packets.   Calling the Soviets a "threat to the Western Hemisphere," the caucus announced that it would be beneficial to "restore the Monroe Doctrine as the cornerstone of American policy in our Hemisphere."6   This new invocation of the Monroe Doctrine has ominous implications for Central America, especially when combined with the virulent anticommunism of the New Right.

Because of its preoccupation with anticommunism and the extension of U.S. geopolitical influence, the New Right downplays and even disregards human rights issues. More accurately, conservatives disregard them if the violations are undertaken by U.S. "friends." Left-wing governments, however, are routinely accused of attacks on both civil and political liberties, and physical and mental integrity. These accusations form the bedrock of the right-wing public opposition to leftist governments.

LIC: A New Right Strategy

The New Right's demand for a new global offensive against communism has resulted not only in the declaration of the Reagan Doctrine but also in the rising prominence of the military doctrine of low intensity conflict (LIC).   It is a developing doctrine promoted by right-wing think tanks such as the National Strategy Information Center and the Center for Strategic and International Studies. (See the Resource Center report: Low Intensity Conflict: The New Battlefield in Central America, April 1986.)

LIC doctrine incorporates many aspects of counterinsurgency strategy and places new emphasis on special operations, covert warfare, psychological operations, military civic action programs, and close coordination between the military and other U.S. agencies like the Agency for International Development (AID).   Two distinctive features of LIC doctrine are its support of counterterrorism strikes and its call for

military operations to recover territory lost to the free world.

LIC strategists contend that the United States is facing a "total grassroots war" supported by the Soviet Union for the purpose of undermining democratic and capitalist values in the third world. To avoid the direct intervention of U.S. troops, which is seen only as a highly undesirable last resort, the United States must fight this subversion in a multidimensional fashion using all available resources.

Unconventional warfare involving Special Operations Forces, mercenaries, and surrogate forces like the contras is one part of low intensity conflict. But the doctrine also advocates expanded civic action programs for the purpose of increasing the influence of the military. LIC proponents also call for deepened Pentagon involvement in "humanitarian assistance" for strategic purposes. Civic action and humanitarian assistance are targeted for communities on the edge of conflicts. Not only must government resources be used but also private ones. At a conference on Special Operations hosted by the National Strategy Information Center, Secretary of the Army John Marsh noted the special role of civilians in low-level war:

> The twilight battlefield of low intensity conflict is an enormous area in which private sector resources can be used. We must find ways to incorporate into a grand strategy the total resources of our society. We live in a nation that has been the global pioneer in industrial development, marketing, advertising, and communications. Now we must harness these restrictions in a commmon security endeavor.[7]

Low intensity conflict strategy also stresses the need to overcome the Vietnam syndrome by mounting a type of psychological operations campaign in the United States to build support for certain kinds of U.S. intervention such as covert wars, surgical counterterrorism strikes, and support of surrogate forces.

Common Ground of Anticommunism

The ideological checkpoints of anticommunism and interventionism provide a gathering place for the Reagan Doctrine's diverse right-wing supporters. Along with the New Right, traditional conservatives and neoconservatives like the editors of the New Republic are marching under the banner of uncompromising anticommunism. Such a common ground is necessary because the counterrevolutionary coalition is by no means monolithic. New Right groups may scrap over territory, tactics, and strategy; their passions, priorities, and resources may vary widely. But they can and do come together in force behind anticommunist interventionism.

Reference Notes

1 Paul Weyrich, "Blue Collar or Blue Blood? The New Right Compared with the Old Right," in Robert W. Whitaker (ed.), The New Right Papers (New York: St. Martin's Press, 1982), p. 53.

2 Ibid, p. 56

3 Robert Armstrong, "Reagan's Uneasy Alliance," NACLA Report on the Americas, July/August 1981, p. 4.

4 NACLA Report on the Americas, July/August 1981, p. 14.

5 Jerry Sanders, "Terminators", Mother Jones, August/September, 1985.

6 "Statement of Principles," The Conservative Caucus.

7 Frank Barnett, B. Hugh Tovar, and Richard Shultz, eds, Special Operations in U.S. Strategy (Washington: National Defense University Press, 1984).

L. Francis Bouchey
Alan Crawford, Thunder on the Right (New York: Pantheon Books, 1980); The Committee of Santa Fe, A New Inter-American Policy for the Eighties (Washington, DC: Council for Inter-American Security, Inc., 1980); Covert Action Information Bulletin, Fall, 1984.

Jeremiah Denton
Official biography provided by Senator Denton.

Roger Fontaine
The Committee of Santa Fe, A New Inter-American Policy for the Eighties (Washington, DC: Council for Inter-American Security, Inc., 1980); Mother Jones, August/September 1985.

Patrick Frawley
Kirkpatrick Sale, Power Shift: The Rise of the Southern Rim and Its Challenge to the Eastern Establishment (New York: Vintage Books, 1975); National Catholic Reporter, October 14, 1983.

Howard Phillips
Alan Crawford, Thunder on the Right (New York: Pantheon Books, 1980); NACLA Report on the Americas, July/August, 1981; Richard A. Viguerie, The New Right: We're Ready to Lead (Falls Church, VA: The Viguerie Co., 1980); The Conservative Caucus, "Ten Years of Progress"; Phone Interview with Russ Bellant, April 21, 1986.

Richard Mellon Scaife
Columbia Journalism Review, July/August, 1981; NACLA Report on the Americas, July/August, 1981.

William E. Simon
Leonard Silk and Mark Silk, The American Establishment (New York: Basic Books, Inc., 1980); Los Angeles Times, December 21, 1980; Accuracy in Media Letterhead; National Catholic Reporter, October 14, 1983; Washington Post, December 27, 1984; Washington Post, May 9, 1985.

Richard Viguerie
Richard A. Viguerie, The New Right: We're Ready to Lead (Falls Church, VA: The Viguerie Co., 1980); Mother Jones, March, 1981; Breakthrough, Spring/Summer, 1985; Washington Post, July 23, 1983; NACLA Report on the Americas, July/August, 1981; Alan Crawford, Thunder on the Right (New York: Pantheon Books, 1980).

Paul Weyrich
Richard A. Viguerie, The New Right: We're Ready to Lead (Falls Church, VA: The Viguerie Co., 1980); NACLA Report on the Americas, July/August, 1981; Alan Crawford, Thunder on the Right (New York: Pantheon Books, 1980); Washington Post, March 22, 1983; Paul M. Weyrich, "Blue Collar or Blue Blood? The New Right Compared with The Old Right," in Robert W. Whitaker (ed.), The New Right Papers (New York: St. Martin's Press, 1982); Correspondence from Council for National Policy, January, 1986.

Part Two

The Central American Connection

In keeping with the "free enterprise" emphasis of the Reagan administration, many private organizations are providing key support for counterrevolutionary wars in Central America. This aid goes primarily to the contras in Honduras but also flows to the Guatemalan and Salvadoran armies for use in their pacification programs in counterinsurgency wars against leftist guerrillas.

New Rightists proclaim that their aid to the contras is an example of a "private-sector solution." "Conservatives have decided to do for the freedom fighters what the American left of the 30s did for the communists in Spain" says Richard Viguerie. But the private nature of this counterrevolutionary support is mostly a matter of appearances. Unlike the private backers of the contras, the Lincoln Brigade and other supporters of the Spanish Republicans were not organized and coordinated by the CIA, White House, or National Security Council. Their support was not shipped on military aircraft and distributed in conjunction with U.S government's own civic action and humanitarian assistance programs. The support movement for the anti-fascists in Spain was not directed by Pentagon advisers and members of the intelligence community. And their contributions were not tax deductible. Moreover, the aid to the Spanish Republicans went to a popularly supported movement, not to a mercenary army.

Type and Quantity of Aid

The exact quantity of private aid that has gone to the contras and other counterrevolutionary forces in Central America is not known. General John Singlaub, the White House designated coordinator of the campaign, has said that the United States Council for World Freedom (USCWF) alone has sent about $500,000 a month over the past two years to the contras. According to L. Francis Bouchey, director of the Council for Inter-American Security, one third of the direct contributions to the contras has been in the form of ammunition and weapons.[1] The balance of private financial support has been non-lethal supplies, including boats, vehicles, food, boots, uniforms, and personal effects.

By late 1985, an estimated $20-$25 million in private aid had been received by the contras—about half of which came from the United States.[2] This estimate does not include the extensive in-kind humanitarian aid distributed by groups like Americares and the Air Commandos to Nicaraguan refugees and to military civic action programs in El Salvador and Guatemala. The Air Commandos alone claim to have distributed $20 million in humanitarian supplies in Central America. In 1986 there have been no signs that this flow of aid has slowed down. In fact, several U.S. contra-support groups have formed within the last year.

Official Coordination of Private Aid

The Reagan administration has been involved in every aspect of the campaign to provide private aid to the contras. The National Security Council has coordinated the private aid campaign to the contras and the Pentagon has helped transport the supplies to Central America. The CIA has guided the political organizing work of the FDN (Nicaraguan Democratic Forces) and the Miskito contra group called MISURA. President Reagan himself has commended the fundraising work of groups like the United States Council for World Freedom. In a letter to one group supporting the Nicaraguan Freedom Fund, the president said that although private aid "cannot take the place of open, direct support from the United States government," it would "complement" official assistance.[3] And when it comes to mercenary support, the administration has looked the other way at blatant violations of the law.

The forces of the New Right, paramilitary organizations, and a number of CIA-linked relief groups have responded enthusiastically to the White House's request for private material support for counterrevolutionary forces in the region. A good deal of the private support comes from individuals who believe they are doing their part to stop the spread of communism or are aiding the victims of communist aggression.

Even before Congress cut off aid to the contras in October 1984, the White House had begun to coordinate private support. Edgar Chamorro, a former FDN director, said that two U.S. officials traveled to rebel camps in the spring of 1984 to assure the contras that the White House would "find a way" to keep them going. Lt. Colonel Oliver North, director of public policy and political/military affairs for the National Security Council (NSC), was one of those officials. The second one was a well-known CIA official. Chamorro said that it was after this visit that the CIA provided funds to publish ads in U.S. papers soliciting private aid for the contras.[4]

Chamorro's account parallels statements made by current and former administration officials to Associated Press reporter Robert Parry. The officials also said that National Security Adviser Robert McFarlane presented a verbal outline on the plan at a presidential briefing in the spring of 1984. Reagan approved the plan, and it was carried out by North, who worked directly under McFarlane.[5] The sources contacted by Parry said the private aid network was started up following congressional protest of the CIA's mining of a Nicaraguan harbor in August 1984.

The Reagan administration needed a figure outside government to coordinate the private fundraising efforts, and it chose retired General John Singlaub. Singlaub's military background and intelligence connections made him the perfect candidate. Singlaub has said he maintains regular communication with "administration contacts" about his contra support efforts. The administration advised him how to structure the campaign within the confines of the laws that bar U.S. citizens from supporting foreign wars. Singlaub told the Miami Herald that high ranking Pentagon officials, including Fred Ikle and Nestor Sanchez (a former CIA associate of Singlaub during the Korean war and currently the DOD's Deputy Assistant Secretary of Inter-American Affairs), helped coordinate his support efforts by arranging military transport of private supplies.[6]

While Singlaub is the main private coordinator of the campaign, Oliver North has been the government's in-house coordinator. He is assisted by right-wing activist Robert Owen, who is paid by the State Department to act as a "consultant" to the contras. North served as a company commander in both conventional and unconventional operations in Vietnam. After the war, he taught at the Marine Corps basic training school and at the FBI academy. In 1981, North was assigned to the NSC, where he was put in charge of "crisis management and counterterrorism assistance planning." In 1983, North was said to have been at the "nerve center" of the planning for the Grenada invasion. North was also the mainstay of the White House Office of Public Liaison's "outreach project" that aimed to build public support for Reagan's Central America policies.

Following the congressional cutoff of covert aid to the contras, NSC assigned North to manage the joint public-private drive to assist the contras. He provided the contras with direct military advice, met frequently with FDN leaders both in Washington and in Central America, and advised private donors how they might contribute to the contras.[7] North also set up logistical supply lines for the contras.

As part of his job, North has worked closely with such groups as the Air Commandos Association, United States Council for World Freedom, and the Citizens for America. In 1985, Representative Vin Weber (R-MN), a leader of the House Conservative Opportunity Society, said North is "in close touch with most of the New Right people."[8]

North has been responsible for the NSC's "perception management" and "psychological warfare operation" designed to manage the way people in the United States and other countries see the Sandinistas. In a February 1984 National Security Decision Document, Reagan directed the NSC, State Department, CIA, and the Pentagon to strengthen ongoing "public diplomacy" projects that manipulated public perception of the war against Nicaragua. The February 1984 directive followed a 1983 Pentagon directive that called for psychological operations aimed to create invasion fears in an attempt to destabilize the government. One official who opposed these psychological operations coordinated by North said, "The idea is to slowly demonize the Sandinista government in order to turn it into a real enemy in the minds of the American people, thereby eroding their resistance to U.S. support for the contras and, perhaps, to a future military intervention in the region."[9]

North's dual role as the NSC's coordinator of private aid to the contras and manager of "public perception" indicates that the effort to provide the contras with private sector support might also be a two-pronged campaign. Not only has the campaign provided valuable assistance to the contras but it also has served as a type of psychological operations aimed to broaden public support for the anti-Sandinista rebels.

Support from the Pentagon and AID

In December 1983, the NSC ordered the Pentagon to transport private humanitarian supplies to Central America on a "space available basis." As a result, military planes carried private supplies to contras several times in 1984. Besides providing free cargo services, the Pentagon has allowed U.S. military bases in Maryland, Michigan, Virginia, and Mississippi to be used as storage spaces for this humanitarian relief. A bill introduced by Senator Jeremiah Denton (R-AL) at the behest of Andy Messing of the National Defense Council and the NSC made this practice legal.

The Pentagon's new role in shipping humanitarian supplies to Central America is just one element of a broader DOD effort to get the military more involved in humanitarian assistance, disaster relief, and civic action programs in Central America. Reflecting this increased interest in nonmilitary aid, the Pentagon in 1985 established an Office of Humanitarian Assistance. This office arranges for the transport of supplies under the provisions of the Denton Amendment while AID administers the program within the region.

Private organizations are not the only ones that have provided humanitarian assistance to the contras. In 1985, Congress approved $27 million in non-lethal aid, which paid for the establishment of another new office called the Nicaraguan Humanitarian Assistance Office. Chris Arcos, a spokesperson for the office, said that the aid was channeled through FDN offices in Miami and New Orleans.

AID has been another source of assistance to the contras. In 1985, two legislators closely tied to the New Right, Representative Bob Livingston (R-LA) and Senator Denton, co-sponsored legislation that authorized AID to earmark $7.5 million to the Miskito Indians living close to the Nicaragua border. This money has been used to support the contras and their families who live in camps and villages within miles of Nicaragua. Roads have been built to facilitate transportation in this sparsely populated area, food is distributed to Nicaraguan refugees, and a radio station is being set up to compete with Radio Sandino. AID channels much of its economic assistance through the Honduran Ministries of Public Works and Health and a New Right group, Friends of the Americas (FOA).

Intelligence Connections

The CIA began organizing contra armies soon after the fall of Somoza. Besides training and providing logistical and financial support to the contras, the CIA has also organized the various political front groups, the latest being the United Nicaraguan Opposition (UNO). Without the covert support offered by the CIA, Nicaragua would not be facing a serious counterrevolutionary threat.   In his statement to the World Court, former FDN political representative Edgar Chamorro, who left the contras because of their human-rights violations, said:

> The FDN turned out to be an instrument of the U.S. government and specifically of the CIA. It was created by the CIA, it was supplied, equipped, armed, and trained by the CIA, and its activities—both military and political—were directed and controlled by the CIA.[10]

In October 1984, Congress barred the CIA from further aiding the contras but the agency secretly has continued to funnel at least several million dollars to the contras. Government officials admitted that the CIA has continued to support the United Nicaraguan Opposition and has paid salaries of rebel officers, FDN fundraising expenses, and the costs of opening FDN offices in Europe and Latin America.[11]

To further assist the contras, the CIA has played a leading role in organizing private support, even to the extent of creating front organizations to receive this aid. According to former FDN leader Edgar Chamorro, the CIA helps the FDN's Adolfo Calero solicit funds inside the United States. "Somebody from the CIA tells him where to go, which door to knock on."

The entire extent of CIA participation in this effort is not publicly known, but from the involvement of numerous members or former members of intelligence organizations the key role of the CIA is obvious. Many of these figures are military men who have long worked for the CIA while others like Ray Cline were civilian members. General Singlaub has acknowledged that he has carried out some CIA functions after the Congress prohibited CIA involvement: "I'll admit that the good many years that I've had serving in the CIA...gives me a feel probably [of] what they were doing, which probably makes me more efficient."[12]

Old Soldiers Take the Lead

Many of the prime movers of the campaign to drum up private support for counterrevolution in Central America are old military men. Many were generals or other high level officers who participated in special operations and unconventional warfare. Their experience in Southeast Asia and their long-time association with the CIA puts them in a position to provide valuable advice about unconventional and counterinsurgency warfare and to act as bridges between the U.S. government and the private sector. According to a report by the staff of the Arms Control and Foreign Policy Caucus:

> The individual driving forces behind the major groups are a small group of about half a dozen men, most of whom have military or paramilitary backgrounds or mercenary experience, and who often participate in more than one organization. For instance, three assistant editors of Soldier of Fortune magazine (which has sent direct aid to the contras) also run or are board members of three other separate groups seeking to aid the contras.

The following are portraits of the main military figures active in U.S. support work for counterrevolution in Central America.

Brigadier General Harry "Heine" Aderholt, USAF (Ret.):

Aderholt is president of the relief organization Air Commandos Association (ACA), whose ranks include retired and active members of Special Operations Forces. Aderholt spent 34 years in the Air Force and for 26 years of his military service he specialized in unconventional warfare operations. In Southeast Asia, Aderholt oversaw special operations in Vietnam, Thailand, and Laos. During a stint at Elgin Air Force Base in Florida, "Heine" Aderholt did studies for Rand Corporation, a CIA-linked think tank. In the early 1960s, he was stationed in Panama where he coordinated civic action programs.

During part of his time in Southeast Asia, Aderholt served as chief of covert air operations under General Singlaub. In Laos, Aderholt coordinated a joint CIA-DOD-AID program to provide "humanitarian relief" to the Hmong (Meo) tribespeople who were organized into a counterrevolutionary mercenary army. For over 20 years, Aderholt has worked closely with World Medical Relief in supplying humanitarian assistance to counterrevolutionary forces.

Aderholt is Soldier of Fortune's unconventional warfare editor. He sits on the boards of Refugee Relief International and the National Defense Council, and was a member of a Special Warfare Panel on Central America formed by the Pentagon in 1984.

Lieutenant Colonel Robert K. Brown (Ret.):

Brown heads the Omega Group which publishes Soldier of Fortune (SOF) and two other gun magazines. Brown, who edits SOF, has personally led training missions to El Salvador. A SOF biography of Brown says he has "reported and advised on war and armies on every continent for more than 20 years."

Known as "Prince Robert" to the SOF staff, Brown claims he initially supported Fidel Castro but turned counterrevolutionary after Castro ousted Batista in 1959. Brown (who wears a T-shirt that shows a skeleton armed with a M-16 in Vietnam above the slogan: "I Was Killing When Killing Wasn't Cool") began his career in the military in

the mid-1950s as an officer with the Army's Counterintelligence Corps. He left the Army in 1957, but he was back in uniform in 1964 to receive training at Fort Benning in the Army Reserve. In 1967, the Army recalled Brown as a captain and trained him for the Special Forces at Fort Bragg. While in Vietnam, Brown worked with the CIA's Phoenix Program of counterterror. The CIA commended him in 1969 for his "outstanding contribution to the Phoenix Program"— a program that executed as many as 40,000 South Vietnamese accused of being members or supporters of the Viet Cong. Brown also served as a commander of a Special Forces team that advised a CIA-formed army of Montagnard tribespeople.

During this period, a State Department official called Brown "one of our leading experts on counterinsurgency." He was

Robert Brown/ Soldier of Fortune, August 1985.

released from active duty in 1970 and remained active in the Army Reserve until 1985 when he retired as a lieutenant colonel.

Past mercenary-related activities include marginal involvement in plots to overthrow Castro and "Papa Doc" Duvalier, recruiting for the Sultan of Oman and the Rhodesian Army, and time spent as a reporter/mercenary in what was then called Rhodesia. As the head of Omega Group, Brown has sponsored numerous military training missions to Central America and delivered military equipment to counterrevolutionary forces in the region. He says he has organized a dozen teams to train the Salvadoran army and loaned nine staffers to teach the contras. "I get to do things that nobody else can," says Brown, "Vacation for me is attacking a fort in Afghanistan."

Lieutenant General Daniel O. Graham (Ret.)

Graham was in charge of army intelligence in Saigon, and was recently accused along with General Westmoreland by a former CIA analyst of participating in a conspiracy to suppress higher enemy troop estimates during the Vietnam War. He served as the director of the Defense Intelligence Agency from 1971 to 1976. In 1977, the South African government secretly paid the Institute of Policy Studies, a University of Miami-based research institute headed by Graham to produce an "independent study" espousing the strategic importance of South Africa to the West. He has served as a military adviser to Reagan.

Graham is currently the director of High Frontier, an organization founded in 1981 and dedicated to the proposition that the United States can be made "safe from attack by Soviet nuclear missiles." He is the chair of the Coalition for the Strategic Defense Initiative. Besides his work promoting Star Wars defense, he is vice-chair of the United States Council for World Freedom, a former staff member of the American Security Council, a member of the Council for National Policy, and is closely associated with the Heritage Foundation.

Major General Edward G. Lansdale (Ret.):

Another old soldier, Lansdale is a prominent figure in promoting low intensity conflict doctrine in Central America. Along with Singlaub and Aderholt, Lansdale was a member of the Special Warfare panel formed by the DOD's Fred Ikle. He is an adviser of the National Defense Council, a group that coordinates private support for counterrevolution in Central America. Lansdale worked simultaneously for the CIA and the Pentagon for over two decades and has long called for closer coordination of military and economic aid programs in counterinsurgency situations.

In the 1950s, Lansdale developed counterinsurgency plans for governments in Vietnam and the Philippines. He was the personal adviser of President Magsaysay of the Philippines and President Diem in South Vietnam. In both countries he developed military civic action programs with the aim of increasing the power and influence of the security forces.

He was a member of the committee in 1959 that wrote the Draper Report which recommended the increased use of civic action programs in the third world. In the early 1960s, Lansdale was involved in several plots to either murder Castro or undermine his public image. In one Pentagon memo, Lansdale referred to the need for the "liquidation of leaders." When not plotting against Castro, Lansdale was assistant to Secretary of Defense Robert McNamara on matters involving the CIA and special operations.

In a recent interview with the Boston Globe, Lansdale called for a broad counterinsurgency program in El Salvador of "psychological operations and civic action in smaller units as a means of giving the El Salvador government a way of going after the [opposition] leaders." Such a program could include "sabotage, if it had a political or military purpose."

Colonel Alexander M. S. McColl:

McColl, who had 11 years of active duty including two tours with the Special Forces in Vietnam, is a colonel with the Army Reserve and also the Military Affairs editor of SOF. While in Vietnam, McColl served under General Singlaub, and it has been reported that he worked for the CIA and Air Force Intelligence. McColl has led at least one SOF team to El Salvador.

Major Andy Messing

An infantry platoon leader in Vietnam who is currently active in the Army Special Forces Reserve, Messing is the most forceful proponent of implementing low intensity conflict doctrine in Central America. Messing has worked under Howard Phillips at The Conservative Caucus, and in 1978 formed the National Defense Council Foundation (NDCF). Current NDCF advisers include Generals Lansdale, Singlaub, and Aderholt, and SOF's Brown has also served as a NDCF adviser. He has close allies in the Conservative Opportunity Society in Washington and counts on support from Senators Denton and Nickles (R-OK).

Messing can be found lobbying in the Capitol, advising the Pentagon, and traveling back and forth to Central America with supplies donated by New Right humanitarians. He is known to have easy access to the National Security Council. Messing persuaded Fred Ikle, Undersecretary of Defense for Public Policy, to form a Special Warfare panel in 1984 to make recommendations of ways the Pentagon could pursue a strategy of low intensity conflict in Central America. Singlaub, who headed that panel, says Messing "serves as my adviser on all matters relating to Congress and the general conservative community."

Until recently, Messing worked for the Pentagon monitoring U.S. intelligence about Central America. Messing has escorted conservative congressional leaders around the low intensity battlefields in Central America. He calls Central America "an accessible laboratory" for the study and implementation of low intensity conflict.

Tom Posey:

A former Marine corporal and a veteran of Vietnam, Posey is the founder of Civilian Materiel Assistance, a mercenary group active in Central America. "I have been a member of numerous right-wing groups all my life," said Posey, "but all they ever did was talk. We formed this group because we

Tom Posey / _Newsweek_, September 17, 1984.

wanted to take the offensive against Communism." Posey, who runs a produce store in Decatur, Alabama, was issued a federal firearms dealers license in 1984 even though he wrote on the application that he planned to send weapons and ammunition to El Salvador at no charge.

Thomas Reisinger:

Reisinger is the president of Refugee Relief International. While in the military, he was the director of the Parachute Medical Rescue Service and served as a medic for the Special forces in Vietnam. He has coordinated Soldier of Fortune relief missions to Laos, Afghanistan, and Central America.

Major General John K. Singlaub (Ret.):

Singlaub, the principal private fundraiser for the contras, began working for the Office of Strategic Services (OSS) during World War II. During his years with OSS, the predecessor agency to both the CIA and the Special Operations Forces, he received military command training and served behind the German lines. He later was transferred to China where he became acquainted with many individuals of the extreme right. He worked for the CIA's China desk and in 1951 was appointed deputy chief of the CIA station in Seoul, Korea. After the Korean war, Singlaub taught at the Army Command and General Staff College and at the Air War College.

In 1966, Singlaub went to Vietnam as the officer in charge of a Special Operations unit that carried out secret missions in Laos, Cambodia, and North Vietnam. In 1968, he became commander of the Joint Unconventional Warfare Task Force that was involved in the Phoenix counterterror program (Singlaub, however, denies being associated with the controversial program). Singlaub personally directed commando units known as "Spike Teams" that fought behind enemy lines. In 1977 Singlaub was relieved of his command in South Korea for publicly criticizing President Carter's plan to withdraw ground troops from the country.

In 1980, Singlaub lectured at the paramilitary training school of the notorious mercenary Mitchell Werbell, and in August 1980 he urged sympathetic understanding of the death squads in Central America. He said that the unwillingness to back military repression in Guatemala "is prompting those who are dedicated to retaining the free enterprise system and continuing their progress toward political and economic development to take matters in their own hands."

Singlaub, a hero to special forces veterans and military adventurers, directs the World Anti-Communist League and the United States Council for World Freedom. Together with his Vietnam war buddy Colonel McColl, Singlaub established the Institute for Regional and International Studies to train third world police and military officers in the methods of counterinsurgency. He has served as the director of education at the American Security Council, is a member of Western Goals and the Council for National Policy, and sits on the board of Refugee Relief International. He was the honorary chair of Ronald Reagan's 1980 campaign for the state of Colorado.

Known as "The General" to his friends, Singlaub is associated with the Special Operations Association (SOA)--self-described as "an elite group of military adventurers who are now conducting or supporting classified 'Special Operations' deep in hostile enemy territory, or have been assigned to United States or foreign units which have conducted such operations." Many SOA members were part of the Studies and Operation Group that Singlaub directed in Vietnam.

Singlaub was asked by the Reagan administration to coordinate private funding for the contras. In this capacity, he works closely with Nestor Sanchez of the DOD, Fred Ikle, and Colonel Oliver North of the National Security Council. Singlaub states his position on Central America clearly: "The concern is that the Sandinistas will spread terrorism into Mexico and the United States by infiltrating trained terrorists into refugee columns that move north. We visualize that if these refugee populations develop into the numbers we project, based upon past experience, states will have to call upon the federal government for troops to maintain law and order and to defend our border. And the only way to meet that need will be by bringing the troops back from Europe." In May 1984, Singlaub was asked by the Pentagon to sit on a panel to make recommendations about military strategy in Central America.

General Richard Stilwell (Ret.): Stilwell, who sits on the board of Americares, has a background both in the military and the CIA. In the early 1960s, he served as the CIA's contact man in the office of the Secretary of Defense and also served as the chief of the Far East Office of Policy Coordination. More recently, Stilwell has been pushing the Pentagon to increase Special Operations Forces in all branches of the military.

Lt. Colonel Gordon Sumner (Ret.): Sumner, the chair of the Council for Inter-American Security, is the former chair of the Inter-American Defense Board (IADB). IADB is an instrument of U.S. policy in Latin America. Its Inter-American Defense College trains Latin American military leaders in military and government affairs. Sumner is a co-author of the Santa Fe Document and served as the chair of the administration's National Bipartisan Commission on Central America.

General David Woellner (Ret.)

The director of CAUSA was an Air Force Special Operations officer in Korea and Vietnam. Since retiring he has been the national director of the Coalition for Peace through Strength and the field director of the American Security Council. His CAUSA biography says he is "currently a special adviser to political and paramilitary groups and representatives of several industrial concerns."

Violating the Neutrality Act with Impunity

In pursuit of its Central America policy, the Reagan administration has not been a stickler for either domestic or international law. An obvious transgression of U.S. law is the support offered by Nicaraguan exiles and U.S. mercenaries to the contra armies. Training camps have been set up in Florida and other states to train paramilitary forces for Central America. Groups like Civilian Materiel Assistance (CMA) and Soldier of Fortune offer military assistance and training, while other organizations provide material support for the Nicaraguan counterrevolutionaries.

This activity appears to be in clear violation of the U.S. Neutrality Act which states:

> Whoever, within the United States, knowingly begins or sets foot or provides or prepares a means for or furnishes the money for, or takes part in, any military or naval expedition or enterprise to be carried on from thence against the territory or dominion of any foreign prince or state, or of any colony, district, or people with whom the United States is at peace shall be fined not more than $3,000 or imprisoned not more than three years, or both.

The origins of the Neutrality Act can be found in the farewell address of George Washington who warned the nation to remain aloof of foreign entanglements. This early commitment to steer a neutral course resulted in the Neutrality Act of 1794.[13]

President Reagan apparently has not enforced this law because of his support for these operations. In the opinion of Representative Michael Barnes (D-MD), "It's all part of the administration's effort to funnel assistance in any manner, even if it circumvents the law, to groups that seek to overthrow the government of Nicaragua."[14]

When asked why he did not enforce the Neutrality Act, President Reagan replied that he would "not want to interfere" with private citizens who help the contras. "I have to say it's quite in line with what has been a pretty well-established tradition in our country."[15]

Not only has the Reagan administration looked the other way at the violations of the Neutrality Act but U.S. government officials have actually encouraged such violations. U.S. officials in El Salvador and Honduras have arranged the initial contacts between U.S. mercenary groups and Central American counterrevolutionary forces. Five agencies—CIA, DOD, FBI, State Department, and Treasury Department—have acknowledged that they have been aware of probable violations of the Neutrality Act but have done nothing to stop these practices.

The Role of Mercenaries

When the Neutrality Act was first enacted, the United States was concerned about protecting its own fragile independence and sovereignty and about getting involved in wars beyond its control. Since then the United States has become less concerned about issues of neutrality and non-intervention. Today, superior U.S. military power is the foundation of U.S. foreign policy. And as one legal authority noted: "In a world where two great powers avoid direct confrontation by sparring for advantage in third world states, supporting opposing sides in internal struggles, the United States has found the Neutrality Act tactically inconvenient."[16]

The United States finds mercenaries and surrogate forces a convenient way to support unpopular counterrevolutionary struggles. Not only does the United States not enforce the Neutrality Act but it now makes routine use of exiles and mercenaries to participate in its covert wars and clandestine operations. In the low-intensity conflict arena, mercenaries are used as surrogate forces as a way of avoiding deployment of U.S. troops.

Mercenaries are soldiers recruited for pay to fight wars that are difficult to support politically in the country in which they fight.[17] Hessian mercenaries were used by King George III in an attempt to crush the American Revolution. During the Vietnam war, the CIA recruited tribespeople to conduct a clandestine war in Laos. And the CIA and U.S. Army recruited mercenaries to fight for the racist Rhodesian government against the successful Zimbabwean liberation forces.

In Central America, contras are essentially a mercenary army that would disintegrate without U.S. official, covert, and private financial and logistical support. Private groups in the United States like Civilian Materiel Assistance and Soldier of Fortune play an important but not essential part in this mercenary effort. They are joined by mercenaries recruited among neo-Nazis in Great Britain and France. Mercenaries receive as much as $2,000 to $10,000 a month, depending on their areas of expertise.[18]

While posing as private military adventurers, these non-Nicaraguan mercenaries operate in close cooperation with the CIA and the U.S. military. Most of them have backgrounds in intelligence and special operations, and many U.S. mercenaries still receive military training as members of national guard and reserve units. The two CMA members shot down in Nicaragua while flying a CIA helicopter had received Ranger special operations training at Fort Bragg shortly before their covert Central American mission. The so-called private soldiers of fortune are often contract employees for the CIA.[19]

Who are These Masked Humanitarians?

Foreign mercenaries, training missions, and the provision of arms represent the most direct private support of counterrevolution. Less direct but still a form of military assistance is the supply of non-lethal items like uniforms, boats, tents, and boots. A more ambiguous type of counterrevolutionary support arrives in Central America as so-called humanitarian assistance to refugees and victims of violence.

The practice of private groups supplying humanitarian assistance like medicine, clothing, and food to counterrevolutionary forces allied with the United States is not a new one. During the Vietnam war, many private voluntary organizations coordinated their aid programs with the Pentagon, the CIA, and the Agency for International Development (AID). Their services supported clandestine CIA armies and military resettlement and strategic hamlet programs. Their private assistance organizations were also used as fronts for intelligence gathering.

In Central America, established private organizations like Project Hope and CARE provide essential support to military-related programs. Both organizations receive AID funds that are then channeled into pacification programs. These traditional humanitarian aid agencies have been joined by a new breed of so-called humanitarian groups. An April 1985 report by the staff of the Arms Control and Foreign Policy Caucus of Congress described these new organizations as "ultra-conservative, even approaching fringe, activist groups."[20]

These New Right humanitarian groups claim that their assistance is purely humanitarian. However, their refusal to coordinate their relief efforts with other refugee and relief organizations (such as the United Nations High Commission on Refugees) and their close association with combatants makes their humanitarian goals highly suspect. Their own statements of support for the contras and the Guatemalan and Salvadoran armies also undermines their reputation as humanitarians.

Helping the Refugees

Groups like Friends of the Americas (FOA) claim that they are humanitarian organizations because they work with refugees in Honduras. But the United Nations High Commission on Refugees, International Red Cross, and World Relief already operate refugee camps in the region. The difference is that FOA and others of its type concentrate their aid directly along the border while the UN and World Relief insist that all their refugee camps be at least 50 kilometers away from the border.

The overwhelming number of refugees who stay along the border are contras or the families of contras. Mario Calero, FDN member and brother of contra leader Adolfo Calero, regards the contras as an army of refugees. He said that the FDN has to take care of over 20,000 refugees. "Some of the refugees are freedom fighters," he said, "I consider myself a refugee."[21] The humanitarian relief provided by the New Right humanitarians permits the contras to maintain their base camps in isolated regions. Without the food, clothing, and medicine supplied by these groups, most Nicaraguan refugees would be forced to move to the established refugee camps, deeper into the interior of Honduras, thereby removing them from the direct control of the contra leaders. In this light, Woody Jenkins, FOA's co-founder, sees his organization's relief effort as a "strategic lever to help the forces of democracy in the region."[22]

KEY INDIVIDUALS AND THEIR CONNECTIONS

	ACA	ASC	Ameri-cares	CC	CBN	CAUSA	TCC	CIS	CNP	FOA	Heri-tage	IRIS	SMOM	NDCF	NFF	NRF	RRII	SOF	USCWF	WGF	WMR
Aderholt	X												X		X	X					X
Bouchey				X	X																
Coors									X		X				X	X			X		
Fontaine				X	X																
Garwood														X					X		
Grace			X						X												
Graham	X			X		X													X	X	
N.B. Hunt						X									X				X	X	
Jenkins					X			X	X						X						
McColl								X					X		X				X		
Messing						X							X						X		
Oschner				X		X		X						X							
Phillips				X		X													X		
Robertson					X	X															
Schlafly						X													X		
Simon		X						X	X	X											
Singlaub	X		X						X				X			X			X	X	

For the New Right humanitarians, there is little difference between refugees and freedom fighters. They give their groups names like the Nicaraguan Refugee Fund and Refugee Relief International as a way of both attracting wider public support and disguising their paramilitary purpose.

Several of the New Right humanitarian groups supporting the contras are fundamentalist religious organizations. Pat Robertson, the head of the powerful Christian Broadcasting Network (CBN), has called the contras "God's army" and said that the United States has a "moral obligation to back the contras." Both Robertson and Jimmy Swaggart have traveled to the Nicaragua border region to preach their fundamentalist gospel and distribute support to anti-Sandinista Nicaraguans.

On a recent mission to the Honduras-Nicaraguan border, Swaggart flew over the villages dropping candy from his plane while his amplified voice drifted over the area. Bonafide relief workers in the region say evangelical groups pop in and out of the area to hand out their donations and propagate their beliefs. Lesser known fundamentalist missions to contra territory include Missions in Motion, Christian Emergency Relief Teams, and Salt and Light—all of which express their desire to care for the victims of communist repression.

The staff report by the Arms Control and Foreign Policy Caucus called into question the humanitarian nature of the aid these groups offer:

> Most groups call their aid 'humanitarian,' but either privately or publicly acknowledge that some of it ends up at contra camps. These groups also have conceded that their 'humanitarian' aid to refugees (which include families of the contras) may indirectly aid the contras by freeing up the contra accounts to purchase weapons and pay combatants.

Partners with the Military

Most of the New Right humanitarian aid supports the contras but a sizeable portion also backs military civic action programs in El Salvador and Guatemala with medical supplies, clothing, and toys. In Guatemala, the military uses the private aid to support its programs of model villages and development poles as part of an effort to pacify the Indian population. The aid to El Salvador is coordinated by the U.S. military mission for use in civic action programs carried out by the Salvadoran army in areas of guerrilla support. The civic action programs in both countries have three objectives: 1) to improve the image of the military , 2) to increase military control in rural areas, and 3) to pacify rebellious communities through psychological operations and social services programs. The United States has encouraged all the armed forces to institute civic action programs. These programs are also called pacification programs, particularly in those countries fighting counterinsurgency wars. Private organizations from the United States assist civic action and pacification programs in Central America by sending down doctors and preachers and by supplying medicine, religious materials, clothing, toys, and other items the armed forces can hand out to the rural population.

The main private supplier of the pacification campaign in El Salvador is the Family Foundation of America (FFA), headed by Dr. Kenneth Wells. Wells, a confidant of the late President Dwight Eisenhower, says that the security provided by the military is a necessary and welcome component of humanitarian assistance. "Self-defense is essential or civic action cannot be carried out," he says. "It provides stability, hope, and the beginning of normalcy to Salvadorans."[23]

A Contradiction in Terms

Bonafide relief organizations are concerned about the political use of humanitarian assistance in Central America. Organizations like Church World Service and Oxfam America feel that the involvement of the Pentagon, the White House, and right-wing anticommunist groups in humanitarian assistance programs undermines true relief and development work by casting suspicion on the motives of all private assistance organizations.[24]

The Geneva Conventions of 1949 and the Protocols of 1977 define humanitarian aid as food, medicine, and clothing. They state that such aid must be given impartially to all sides in a conflict to relieve human suffering, and it must be provided only to civilians or combatants who are sick, wounded, or shipwrecked. Under these international conventions, assistance to military forces cannot be designated "humanitarian."

The vast majority of assistance provided by the new private groups in Central America violates these guidelines. Aid to the contras and their families and support of military civic action programs is paramilitary in nature. Whether the assistance is food, army boots, or Christmas gift packages, it should be considered paramilitary because it either directly supports combatants or is discriminately provided to civilians on only one side of the conflict. Similarly, U.S. government "humanitarian assistance" to the contras must rightfully be designated as being paramilitary in nature. Commenting on the political and paramilitary use of aid, Joseph Mitchell, former director of the AID Office of U.S. Foreign Disaster Assistance, said, "Congressional advocates evidently believe that humanitarian aid to combatants engaged in a civil war is somehow different from aiding them militarily as if food, clothing and shelter are not rations, uniforms and tents."[25]

A Tax-Exempt Counterrevolution

Private support of the contras and other counterrevolutionary forces in Central America is often tax exempt. Contributions to organizations like the United States Council for World Freedom (USCWF), the Nicaraguan Freedom Fund, and the Nicaraguan Development Council are regarded as charitable donations because they go to organizations that enjoy tax-exempt status with the Internal Revenue Service. New Right think tanks and lobbying groups—many of which serve as contra support groups—benefit from the same status.

Singlaub's USCWF received tax-exempt status in October 1982. The Los Angeles IRS office had referred USCWF's application to

Tax Exempt Organizations

New Right Humanitarian and Contra Support Groups

Air Commando Association	Institute for Regional and International Studies
American Foundation for Resistance International	International Aid
Americares	International Relief Friendship Foundation
Caribbean Commission	Knights of Malta
Christian Broadcasting Network	National Defense Council Foundation
Council for National Policy	Nicaraguan Development Council
Tom Dooley Foundation InterMed USA	Nicaraguan Freedom Fund
Eagle Forum	Nicaraguan Refugee Fund
Family Foundation of America	Refugee Relief International
Friends of the Americas	U.S. Council for World Freedom
Human Development Foundation	World Medical Relief

Think Tanks and Public Pressure Groups

Accuracy in Academia	Council for the Defense of Freedom
American Enterprise Institute	Free Congress Foundation
American Security Council	Heritage Foundation
Committee on the Present Danger	Liberty Foundation
Concerned Citizens for Democracy	National Endowment for the Preservation of Liberty
The Conservative Caucus	Western Goals

IRS, Cumulative List of Organizations Described in Sec 170(c) of the Internal Revenue Code of 1954, (1986); Phone interviews.

Washington, noting that there were "no precedents" for such a group receiving tax exempt status as either a charitable or educational organization. In August 1982, in response to a question from IRS headquarters in Washington, Albert T. Koen, who was then the council's treasurer, wrote that "at no time will the USCWF ever contemplate providing materiel or funds to any revolutionary, counterrevolutionary or liberation movement." His statement contrasted sharply with a clause in USCWF's constitution that pledges the organization to provide "material support to liberation movements."

Asked about the letter in August 1985, Koen said he considered the pledge to apply only to the shipment of weapons to insurgent groups, not to the sending of nonlethal supplies. Dictionaries define "materiel" as supplies and tools needed for any work or enterprise, and more specifically as weapons, equipment, and supplies needed by armed forces. Johnnie Johnson, Koen's successor as council treasurer, said the aid was proper because it the "blessing of the [U.S.] government."[26]

Corporate America Joins the Cause

In the eyes of the contra supporters, the Nicaraguan counterrevolutionaries are not only fighting for freedom and democracy but also for capitalism and free enterprise. Seeing their own interests threatened by revolution in Central America, many corporations and business owners have put their money behind the contras. As Malcolm Forbes, editor of *Forbes* business magazine, has said: "For moral and strategic reasons, Congress had better vote for a healthy flow of support for the contras. Their fight is our fight, too."[27]

Asked how the rebels had received weapons after Congress cut off CIA assistance in 1984, USCWF director Singlaub said the anti-Sandinista forces had raised money for arms from Latin American governments and from private corporations and individuals in Western Europe. "Those funds are deposited in banks overseas, from which they get letters of credit to buy on the international arms market the weapons that they need....I think the European money is

coming from corporations that had their properties in Nicaragua expropriated or nationalized or which withdrew....I don't know whether the corporations as an entity have done it or whether the officers of corporations have contributed. In this country, when I go to people, it's the individuals that make the contribution rather than any corporation." In addition, an American "could write a check and send it to one of these overseas accounts." Most of this non-U.S. military aid has come from Israel, El Salvador, Honduras, Taiwan, and South Korea.[28] The FDN has also said that it has received "financial injections" for arms from private groups in West Germany, Japan, England, and Holland.[29]

The FDN's Mario Calero said that well-known U.S. corporations provide funds sometimes laundering the money through paper organizations in Panama and other countries. General Singlaub, said that he frequently approaches companies that have done business in Nicaragua or hope to invest there in the future.[30] Another fundraiser for the contras said that "fundraising efforts have paid off best with people who used to work in the government and who are now in corporations with defense contracts."[31]

Pharmaceutical companies head the list of the major contributors to New Right humanitarian groups active in the region. These include: GD Searle, Sterling Drug, Merck & Company, and Richardson Vicks.[32] Other corporations, including Curt Messex, Northrop, and Emery Air Freight, have donated to groups like the Air Commandos and Refugee Relief International for humanitarian relief in Central America.[33] Company owners, like John Howell of Howell Instruments and Lew Lehrman of Rite-Aid, have funded contra support groups, while high corporate executives from Standard Oil, InterNorth, and Western Geophysical were among those attending a fundraising dinner for the contras and their families.

Until the recent plunge in petroleum prices, a steady source of funding for New Right groups active in Central America has come from the wealthy oil men and women of Texas, including the owners of small companies like Parrott Oil and First Texas Royalty & Exploration. The Hunt brothers

(Nelson Bunker and Herbert) have contributed and offered their personal support at events like the Freedom Fighters' Banquet hosted by the World Anti-Communist League.

Another major business figure linked with counterrevolutionary efforts in Central America is Rich DeVos of Amway. A governor of the Council for National Policy and a board member of the National Endowment for Democracy, a quasi-private organization funded by the U.S. Information Agency, DeVos has apparently allowed Amway distributorships to be used to collect "Shoe Boxes for Liberty." In addition, Amway consumer products have been distributed in Guatemala and Honduras by humanitarian groups.34 Amway, however, has denied that it financially supports the contras.

Wealthy individuals do more than send small relief packages to the contras. Ellen Garwood, heir to the Clayton Anderson fortune, has contributed large sums to groups like the United States Council for World Freedom and the National Defense Council, including much of the amount necessary to buy a helicopter. A FDN representative said that one wealthy U.S. businessman had donated money for anti-aircraft missles and that another person had recently purchased a large cargo plane to ferry supplies to Central America.35

Two major corporate figures stand out for their large financial support to the cause of anticommunism: Joseph Coors and J. Peter Grace.

Joseph Coors and Family

The Coors family, which has a history of funding extremists groups like the John Birch Society, is a major source of funds for both the think tanks and the pressure and propaganda groups of the New Right. The family's wealth stems from the Colorado-based Coors Company, the country's fifth largest brewery, which was founded by Adolph Coors, a poor German immigrant who died in a fall from a hotel window in 1929. His sons, Joseph and Bill, now run the company with the help of their sons.

Besides brewing beer, the Coors Company also manufactures alumina and oxide ceramics, owns a rice milling business, and has an oil exploration and development business. Its subsidiaries include: Cadco, Coors Distributing, Coors Biotech Products, Coors Biomedical, Coors Energy, American Center for Occupational Health, Rocky Mountain Water, Coors Food Products, and RI Ceramics. Since 1978, labor unions, minority groups, and women's organizations have participated in a boycott against Coors beer because of the racist, sexist, and anti-labor policies of the Coors family.

In 1984, a statement by Bill Coors to a group of Black business owners added more fuel to a national boycott campaign against Coors beer. Coors said that "one of the best things they (slave traders) did for you is to drag your ancestors over here in chains." Bill Coors also said that the main problem with Blacks was that they "lack the intellectual capacity to succeed."

Joseph Coors is the financial angel who stands behind the Heritage Foundation, Free Congress Foundation, and Citizens for America. Through those groups, Coors has helped establish the New Right's political agenda and philosophy. Coors is also a major funder of right-wing religious groups including the Church League of America, Fellowship of Christian Athletes, Moral Majority, and Campus Crusade for Christ. Holly Coors was a Philadelphia socialite before marrying Joseph in 1941. She is a member of the board of regents of the CBN University, director of the Citizens for America, and is active in New Right circles. She lists her role models as Nancy Reagan and Jeane Kirkpatrick.

Money from the Coors family also flows into such groups as the Nicaraguan Freedom Fund, U.S. Council for World Freedom, Council for National Policy, and the Nicaraguan Refugee Fund. According to the leader of a civilian commando unit supporting the contras, "Coors Brewery is one of the contras' biggest supporters."

J. Peter Grace

J. Peter Grace heads the WR Grace Company, a $6.7 billion-a-year conglomerate that owns subsidiaries involved in chemical production, fertilizer production, animal husbandry, restaurants (Carrows, Taco Villa, and other chains), coal mining, oil drilling, book distribution, sporting goods, western wear, and jewelry. The company has subsidiaries in over 37 countries, ranks as the 53rd largest U.S. corporation on the Fortune 500 list, and paid no taxes from 1981 through 1983 because of assorted tax breaks.

Its board members include: Roger Milliken (chair of Milliken & Company and a large contributor to right-wing groups including Western Goals), Robert Macauley (director of Americares and founder of Virginia Fibre), George Jenkins (Chair of Metropolitan Life Insurance), and Fredrich Karl Flick (partner of Flick Industries).

WR Grace is more than 30 percent owned by the Flick Financial Group, a consortium of German businessmen. The Flick Group funded the Nazi's rise to power in pre-war Germany. Frederick Flick, former leader of the Flick Group, was convicted by the Nuremberg Tribunal and sentenced to seven years in prison for "slave labor, plunder, and spoilation." Even before the Flick family bought 30 percent of his company, Grace had hired a number of ex-Nazi scientists and technicians who came to the United States.

Another connection with the Nazis is Dr. Otto Ambros, a brilliant scientist who worked during the war with I.G. Farben Company, the firm that developed the Zyklon-B gas used in the extermination camps. The Nuremberg Tribunal convicted Ambros of mass murder and slavery for his role in providing Farben with 200,000 laborers from the Auschwitz concentration camp. In 1958, Grace petitioned the U.S. ambassador in Germany to allow Ambros to emigrate to the United States. Grace said that he admired Ambros "not only for his ability but—more important—for his character" and hired him as a technical adviser for the company.

President Kennedy in 1961 asked Grace to head the Commerce Department Committee on the Alliance for Progress, which predictably recommended more U.S. aid to the private sector and more government encouragement for U.S. foreign investment. The same year Grace became a founding father to the American Institute of Free Labor Development (AIFLD), a CIA-linked organization funded by the Agency for International Development (AID) that promotes pro-U.S. labor unions in Latin America. Grace, who chaired AIFLD until 1980, said, "AIFLD urges cooperation between labor and management and an end to class struggle." Former CIA agent Philip Agee wrote that Grace has been "a front man for CIA labor operations." In the early 1960s, the Grace Foundation contributed to the Citizens for a Free Cuba, AIFLD, American Council for the International Promotion of Democracy Under God, and Radio Free Liberty.

More recently, Grace chaired President Reagan's Private Sector Survey on Cost Control (known as the Grace Commission). He is a board member of the Friends of the Democratic Center in Central America (PRODEMCA), an organization that is funded by the United States Information Agency and which supports the contras.

J. Peter Grace heads Americares and the Knights of Malta, two groups that channel aid to support counterrevolution in Central America. WR Grace official Fred Bona acknowledged that J. Peter Grace "may have asked" the Central America chapters of the Knights of Malta to help distribute aid to Nicaraguan refugees in Honduras.

WR Grace maintains close relations with the anti-Sandinista leader of the Catholic Church in Nicaragua, Cardinal Miguel Obando y Bravo. Obando y Bravo has sought aid from Grace for development programs designed to "thwart the Marxist-Leninist policies of the Sandinistas." In a conversation asking for support from the company, the cardinal said that his leadership represents "the best organized opposition in Nicaragua to the present government's effort to change the country into a Marxist-Leninist society." The company says its donations to Obando y Bravo are in the form of "rosaries and films."

Reference Notes

1 Newsweek, August 26, 1985.
2 Newsweek, August 26, 1985.
3 Miami Herald, June 16, 1985.
4 Miami Herald, June 24, 1985.
5 Washington Post, October 8, 1985; Village Voice, October 2, 1985.
6 Miami Herald, June 24, 1985.
7 New York Times, July 8, 1985.
8 Washington Post, August 11, 1985.
9 Knight-Ridder Newspapers, November 24, 1985.
10 Congressional Record, January 30, 1986.
11 St. Louis Post-Dispatch, April 14, 1986
12 Common Cause, September/October 1985.
13 For an excellent discussion of the Neutrality Act, see: Jules Lobel, "The Rise and Decline of the Neutrality Act," Harvard International Law Journal, Summer 1983.
14 New York Times, September 10, 1984.
15 Washington Post, October 27, 1984.
16 Lobel, op. cit.
17 Covert Action Information Bulletin, Fall 1984.
18 Latin American Weekly Report, June 21, 1985, citing reports in the anti-Nazi monthly Searchlight and the Israeli trade union confederation daily Davar.
19 See Covert Action Information Bulletin, Fall 1984.
20 "Report by the staff of the Arms Control and Foreign Policy Caucus," House of Representatives, April 23, 1985.
21 Sojourners, October 1985.
22 Village Voice, June 18, 1985.
23 Soldier of Fortune, March 1986.
24 National Catholic Reporter, January 1, 1985.
25 Oxfam Legislative Update, March 1986.
26 New York Times, August 27, 1985.
27 Forbes, February 25, 1985.
28 Washington Post, October 8, 1985.
29 Latin American Weekly Report, June 21, 1985.
30 Texas Observer, September 27, 1986.
31 The Nation, March 9, 1985.
32 Washington Post, December 27, 1984.
33 ACA Newsletter, May 1985.
34 Wall Street Journal, June 14, 1985; Synapses, "The Christian Broadcasting Network: Unholy Alliances," undated.
35 Miami Herald, January 21, 1985.

Harry Aderholt

The Metro Times, October 9, 1985; Soldier of Fortune, August 1985; The Nation, November 2, 1985: Boston Globe, December 30, 1985.

Robert Brown

William Turner, Power on the Right, (Berkeley: Ramparts Press, 1971); Covert Action Information Bulletin, Fall 1984; Soldier of Fortune, August 1985; Time, August 9, 1985.

Daniel Graham

Washington Post, January 1, 1984; Counterspy, August-October, 1981; The National Reporter, Winter 1985.

Edward Lansdale

Boston Globe, December 30, 1984; L. Fletcher Prouty, The Secret Team: The CIA and Its Allies in Control of the United States and the World (New Jersey: Prentice-Hall, 1973); Peter Dale Scott, "Exporting Military-Economic Development: America and the Overthrow of Sukarno, 1965-67," in Malcolm Caldwell, ed., Ten Years' Military Terror in Indonesia (Nottingham: Spokesman Books, 1975); Daniel Schorr, Clearing the Air (Boston: Houghton Mifflin, 1977); Konstantin Tarasov and Vyacheslav Zubenko, The CIA in Latin America (Moscow: Progress Publishers, 1984); Alfred W. McCoy, The Politics of Heroin in Southeast Asia (New York: Harper & Row, 1972).

Alexander McColl

Boston Globe, December 30, 1985; Soldier of Fortune, August 1985; Village Voice, October 1, 1985; Covert Action Information Bulletin, Fall 1984.

Andy Messing

The Nation, November 2, 1985; Village Voice, November 26, 1985.

Tom Posey

National Catholic Reporter, May 24, 1984.

Thomas Reisinger

Soldier of Fortune, August 1985.

John Singlaub

Times of London, September 15, 1985; New Republic, September 30, 1985; Boston Globe, December 30, 1984; COHA, October 30, 1980, "Controversial Reagan Campaign Links With Guatemalan Goverment and Private Sector Leaders"; Village Voice, October 22, 1985.

Richard Stilwell

L. Fletcher Prouty, The Secret Team: The CIA and Its Allies in Control of the United States and the World (New Jersey: Prentice-Hall, 1973); Joseph Burkholder Smith, Portrait of a Cold Warrior (New York: G.P. Putnam's Sons, 1976).

Gordon Sumner

The Nation, May 21, 1977.

Joseph Coors

Saturday Evening Post, April 1985; Life, March 1985; Labor Report on Central America, September/October, 1985; Miami Herald, June 24, 1985; Los Angeles Times, May 25, 1985; Washington Post, March 29, 1984.

J. Peter Grace

May 9, 1984, memorandum from company official J.J. Meehan to J. Peter Grace recommending support for Obando y Bravo; Miami Herald, June 24, 1985; National Catholic Reporter, October 14, 1983; Los Angeles Times, April 24, 1982; Public Citizen, August 1985; The National Reporter, Summer 1985; Penny Lernoux, The Cry of the People (New York: Doubleday, 1980).

Part Three

New Right Policymakers

American Enterprise Institute
Washington, DC

Principals: Paul W. McCracken (president).

The American Enterprise Institute was founded in 1943 by Lewis H. Brown, chair of the Johns-Mansville Company, to promote free enterprise ideas. A non-profit organization, AEI receives extensive financial support from drug-related foundations such as the Smith Richardson and Lilly Foundations.

Primarily concerned with developing an ideological defense of capitalism, the Institute serves as a meeting place for various blocs of the Reagan administration. While she was a resident scholar with AEI, Jeane Kirkpatrick wrote the essay on "Dictatorships and Double Standards" that brought her to the attention of Ronald Reagan. Her essay drew a distinction between "authoritarian" and "totalitarian" governments, and has been used as the rationale for Reagan administration alliances with right-wing dictatorships.

AEI has served as a recruitment pool for the administration and for the New Right humanitarians. AEI resident scholars who later joined the Reagan administration include: David Stockman (Office of Management and the Budget), James C. Miller (who replaced Stockman at OMB), William Brock (Secretary of Labor), Fred Ikle (Undersecretary of Defense for Public Policy), Vice President George Bush, Roger Fontaine (former member of the National Security Council), and Jeane Kirkpatrick (former UN Ambassador). Ikle, Fontaine, and Kirkpatrick have been key figures in the formula-

tion of the Reagan foreign policy in Central America. William Simon was an AEI associate during the late 1970s. He currently serves as the chair of the Nicaraguan Freedom Fund and is a member of Americares and the Knights of Malta. Another AEI associate, Michael Novak, is also on the board of directors of the Nicaraguan Freedom Fund. Neo-conservative ideologue and ardent anti-Sandinista Irving Kristol has also been associated with AEI.

American Security Council (ASC)
Boston, VA

Principals: John Fisher (founder and president, chair of Coalition for Peace through Strength), Elbridge Dubrow, Steve Donchess (Secretary), Harold Falk, (Treasurer), Robert Perry, Greg Hilton, Sam Dickens (Coordinator of Latin American affairs), Robert W. Galvin (Motorola), James Angleton (former CIA), General Singlaub, Ray Cline, Admiral Elmo Zumwalt (ret.), Dr. Scott Thompson (former USIA), Edwin Feulner, Jr. (Heritage Foundation).

The American Security Council is the political action arm of the American Security Council Foundation and serves as a voice of the military industrial complex. It is engaged in lobbying, produces cold war propaganda, and sponsors a number of related institutes including the Freedom Studies Center ("the private West Point of psycho-political warfare"), the American Foreign Policy Institute, and the Coalition for Peace through Strength.

A key figure in the founding of ASC (known originally as the Mid-West Library) in 1955 was General Robert E. Wood, the chair of

Sears Roebuck. It was founded at the height of the McCarthy era to investigate "questionable organizations" and provide intelligence services to corporations. John M. Fisher, who was on loan to Sears from the FBI as a "personnel consultant," was the organization's prime organizer. Modeled after the FBI's dossier system, the ASC service helped member firms identify and weed out employees who were considered disloyal to the free enterprise system. By the early 1970s, ASC had accumulated the names of more than one million individuals and organizations in its files.

ASC promotes a tough military policy founded on hard-line anticommunism. According to an ASC brochure, "The cold war is a psychological hot war, waged by communism to shape and influence the actions of free men." ASC activities include advertising campaigns, radio appeals, film-making, and fundraising. One ASC production, a film documentary entitled "Attack on the Americas," raised a shrill cry of alarm about creeping communist influence in Central America. Air Force Colonel Samuel T. Dickens of the Council for Inter-American Security coordinated the production of the documentary.

ASC's corporate supporters include General Electric, Lockheed, Motorola, General Dynamics, Quaker Oats, Honeywell, U.S. Steel, Kraft Foods, Stewart-Warner, Schick-Eversharp, Sears Roebuck, and Boeing.

ASC has forged close connections between the right wing in Central America and anticommunist U.S. generals. In 1979, retired Generals Singlaub (ASC's director of education) and Graham headed an ASC delegation to Guatemala in order to establish links with the Guatemalan right. Host for the delegation was Guatemalan plantation owner Roberto Alejos, member of the extreme right wing and director of the Knights of Malta. The itinerary for the visit included meetings with then-president General Romeo Lucas Garcia and the Guatemalan military high command. The trip also included helicopter tours to inspect rural counterinsurgency areas.

In 1983, President Reagan made a speech to the annual convention of the Veterans of Foreign Wars in which he called for support of the Nicaraguan contras. Shortly afterwards, the VFW membership voted to set up a fund for non-military aid to the rebels which would be administered by ASC. The VFW said it raised about $5000 for the contras which it subsequently handed over to ASC and which, according to the Council, was then sent to the International Committee of the Red Cross. The Red Cross denies receiving the money.

In 1981, ASC sponsored a trip by Roberto D'Aubuisson to visit congressional leaders in Washington. The next year the Council covered the expenses of a trip by contra leader Steadman Fagoth to testify before congress. ASC also uses its "Voter Index," which rates congress members on their defense votes, to select congressional districts to be targeted for radio appeals on support for the contras. In April, 1985, ASC sponsored a "Why Should We Support the Freedom Fighters" fundraising dinner. The event honored Jeane Kirkpatrick and featured FDN leaders. ASC has paid for full-page newspaper ads supporting aid for the contras.

Center for Strategic and International Studies (CSIS)
Washington, DC

Principals: Robert Kupperman (senior associate), Edward Luttwak (expert on low intensity conflict), Ray Cline (former Deputy Director for Intelligence of the CIA).

Founded in 1962 and affiliated with Georgetown University, this conservative think tank specializes in U.S. national security and foreign policy. Increasingly prominent in foreign policy studies, CSIS theories of a Soviet-coordinated terrorist network became part of the motif of the Reagan administration. CSIS works closely with the Pentagon in developing military doctrine and operational strategy.

In 1984, CSIS published a book entitled Strategic Requirements for the Army to the Year 2000 that, among other things, examined such topics as "counterterrorism," "unconventional war," "low intensity conflict," and "the future of U.S. foreign and defense policy." The book advocated that the U.S. Army adapt its doctrine and training to meet the needs of "low-intensity, unconventional, and proxy conflict in non-European areas."

Several individuals associated with the CSIS have been involved in the Reagan administration or in its counterrevolutionary programs. Richard Allen, the administration's first National Security Adviser, was co-founder of CSIS. Latin America specialist to the National Security Council, Roger Fontaine, was also associated with CSIS. Henry Kissinger and Alexander Haig have also been resident specialists at CSIS. Arnaud de Borchgrave, editor of the Washington Times, is a former CSIS fellow. Edward Luttwak, CSIS's scholar in low intensity conflict, served on the Special Warfare Panel created by Undersecretary of Defense Fred Ikle in 1984.

Committee for the Free World
New York, NY

Principals: Midge Decter.

Formed in 1981, this right-wing group holds yearly conferences and provides other exchanges for "anticommunist intellectuals from around the world." It receives most of its funding from the Scaife and Olin Foundations.

Several panelists at a Committee forum in December 1985 included leading neo-conservatives and members of the Reagan administration, including Richard Pipes of the Committee on the Present Danger and a member of the National Security Council; Assistant Secretary of Defense Richard Perle, who is also a member of the Committee on the Present Danger; Assistant Secretary of State Elliott Abrams (son-in-law of Midge Decter); and Norman Podhoretz, husband of Midge Decter and editor of the neo-conservative journal Commentary. At the conference, neo-conservative panelist Irving Kristol called for increased support for anticommunist "freedom fighters" around the globe. He said that even "small defeats" would shake up the "Soviet regime," and suggested that the "reformation of the Marxist-Leninist system" should be the central goal of U.S. foreign policy.

Committee on the Present Danger
Washington, DC

Principals: Paul Nitze (founder), Ray Cline, Daniel Graham, Jeane Kirkpatrick, Eugene Rostow, Richard Allen (Reagan's former National Security Adviser), Richard Pipes, William Casey.

Called the "classiest of the hard-line think tanks," the Committee on the Present Danger is so far right that it calls its former member, Ronald Reagan, a moderate. It was founded in 1977 by several die-hard conservatives who led a committee of the same name in the late 1940s and 1950s. The Committee is an elite, policy-pushing group which stays in the background and restricts its interests to U.S.-Soviet relations. Increased military spending is and has always been its main demand. The Committee supplied a full 50 of its members to the Reagan administration, including Jeane Kirkpatrick and Defense Secretary Caspar Weinberger.

THE CONSERVATIVE CAUCUS, INC.

National Headquarters
450 Maple Avenue East
Vienna, Virginia 22180
(703) 893-1550

·1974-1986·

The Conservative Caucus (TCC)
Vienna, Virginia

Principals: Howard Phillips.

TCC was founded in 1976 because, in the opinion of its founders, "both political parties in Washington, DC had surrendered control to bureaucratic, liberal special interests." Now boasting 600,000 members, this tax-exempt organization considers itself a nationally organized grassroots lobby. Through action at the congressional district level, it seeks to influence federal policy on a variety of issues. It coordinates the activities of the "far-flung ad hoc 'home and family' groups" like Moral Majority, and has also mobilized opposition to the Panama Canal Treaties and SALT II. Its publications include the monthly Conservative Manifesto and the quarterly Grassroots. TCC utilizes a variety of grassroots mobilizing techniques, including direct mail appeals, advertising campaigns, radio and TV spots, billboard campaigns, and phone banks.

Regarding Central America, TCC works to restore the Monroe Doctrine and employs assorted "vehicles" to "eliminate Soviet military power from our once peaceful neighborhood." In March, 1984, Caucus chairman Howard Phillips testified to Congress about policy directions in Central America. Calling Nicaragua an "expansionist, fascist colonial proxy regime," he said the U.S. must have the objective of replacing "by whatever means necessary, the Communist junta which reigns by terror in Managua." The TCC in conjunction with the Friends of the Americas, Committee for the Survival of a Free Congress, National Defense Council, and 15 corporations was involved in sending a cargo of aid packages, called "Shoe Boxes for Liberty", to the contras. The Mississippi National Guard transported the shipment in May 1984 at the request of Senator Jeremiah Denton. TCC has promoted a Western Goals' campaign to aid the contras.

Many prominent figures in the New Right support TCC. Andy Messing worked as Howard Phillips' right-hand man at TCC in 1979. The organization cites firm support for its program from General Singlaub, General Graham, Senators Orrin Hatch, Jesse Helms, and Jeremiah Denton. In his keynote address at TCC Tenth Anniversary Banquet, Senator Helms said: "I want The Conservative Caucus members across the country to know that if I ever have to select the group I will take my stand with at Armageddon...You are the group."

Council for the Defense of Freedom
Washington, DC

Principals: Marx Lewis (chair), Don Irvine (treasurer).

This extreme anticommunist group used to call itself the Council Against Communist Aggression, but changed its name around 1980. Founded in 1951, its 6200 members include trade union officers, business

leaders, clergy, educators, journalists, and academic experts. Its only criteria for membership is a commitment to "combating communist aggression and insuring national security." The Council has spawned two watchdog groups, Accuracy in Media (AIM) and Accuracy in Academia (AIA), which have shown a strong interest in Central America.

Council publications include a weekly newspaper, the Washington Inquirer, which is circulated in Congress. The Inquirer's National Committee list reads like a roster of the congressional New Right, including Representatives Philip Crane, Bill Hefner, Bob Stump, William Dannemeyer, and Trent Lott, and Senators Jesse Helms and Jeremiah Denton. Frank Barnett, president of the National Strategy Information Center, also serves on the committee.

AIM, founded in 1969 by Reed Irvine, calls itself "America's media watchdog," and sees its mission as combating media "misinformation" and "distortion." AIM's advisory board and executive officer list includes several New Right humanitarians, including Midge Decter and William Simon, both with the Nicaraguan Freedom Fund. Also on the list is Texas heiress Ellen Garwood, who bought a helicopter for the contras, and is a frequent contributor to their cause. The Council's other progeny, Accuracy in Academia, was founded after Reed Irvine concluded that reporters were so "liberal" because they were "the products of our liberal arts colleges."

Council for Inter-American Security (CIS)
Washington, DC

Principals: Ronald F. Docksai (president), L. (Lynn) Francis Bouchey (executive vice-president), David C. Jordan, Lewis Tambs (ambassador to Costa Rica), Robert Emmet

Moffit (founding director and former Senior Legislative Assistant for Foreign Affairs), Gordon Sumner (chair, principal adviser of the Presidential Bipartisan Commission on Central America Affairs), Andy Messing, Francis Graves (Republican National Committee).

Founded in 1976 and now claiming 70,000 members, this influential group has provided both policy and policymakers to the Reagan administration. CIS sponsors educational programs, seminars, conferences, briefing sessions, and public information campaigns on defense-related issues.

One of its reports, A New Inter-American Policy for the Eighties, known as the Santa Fe Document, contributed to the foundation of Reagan administration policies in Central America. Written by CIS members L. Frances Bouchey, Roger Fontaine, David Jordan, Gordon Sumner, and Lewis Tambs, the report claimed that the United States was "engaged in World War III," and reminded its readers that "in war there is no substitute for victory." Describing Central America as "the soft underbelly of the United States," the report called for restoration of the Monroe Doctrine as the basis of U.S. policy in the region. It recommended increased military ties with "friendly" Central American governments, the provision of military training and assistance programs, and both technical and psychological assistance programs to help those countries fight "terrorism."

CIS members have called for the removal of the Sandinista government in Managua. Executive Vice-President Bouchey has said there is "no long-term possibility for peace" as long as the Sandinistas are in power. He says he wants "the administration and Congress to do whatever is necessary to remove the Sandinista regime." Bouchey is one of several CIS members who have formed connections with other right-wing groups. Organizer and chair for several CAUSA conferences (See CAUSA profile in Part Three), he was commissioned by the Reverend Sun Myung Moon's World Media Conference to prepare and present a "content analysis" of the New York Times and Washington Post coverage of U.S. policy in El Salvador.

Top CIS officials "shuttle to and from key policy-making and advisory roles" in the administration. Lewis Tambs, for instance, served as a consultant to the National Security Council and is now ambassador to Costa Rica. Gordon Sumner, former chair of the Inter-American Defense Board, acted as special consultant to the State Department's Bureau of Inter-American Affairs. Patrick J. Buchanan became Reagan's communications director, and the ubiquitous Roger Fontaine, who also has ties to the Moon organization, served as Latin America specialist for the National Security Council.

In March 1985, the Council held a "Nicaraguan Freedom Gala," at the Beverly Wilshire Hotel in Beverly Hills. The event, which raised $8000 for the anti-Sandinista rebels, featured contra leaders Fernando Chamorro and Steadman Fagoth. CIS planned to use some of the money for radio spots featuring excerpts from a speech by President Reagan which called for aid to the contras. The rest of the money was to be used to produce a TV documentary called "Central America: Before It's Too Late," and to conduct a media blitz of 50 congressional districts whose elected representatives were considered swing votes on the contra issue. The Council also promoted the "Shoe Boxes for Liberty" campaign through its newsletter, West Watch.

Council for National Policy (CNP)
Washington, DC

Principals: (See box)

More than any other group, CNP represents the entire spectrum of the New Right, bringing together corporate executives, religious leaders, legislators, former high government and military figures, and activists. CNP, an elite New Right policy formulation group, was formed in 1981 by Nelson Bunker Hunt, Herbert Hunt, and another Texas millionaire T. Cullen Davis. It is a highly secretive group of 200 members that discusses public policy issues at quarterly meetings. Officers and members include many wealthy business owners, five congressional representatives, numerous state and local government officials, representatives of other New Right organi-

Council for National Policy

(a selected listing of the Board of Governors)*

Dr. Frank Aker
Lt. Commander
U.S. Navy
Quantico, VA

Pat Boone
Entertainer
Los Angeles, CA

Hon. Othal Brand
Mayor
McAllen,TX

Patrick Buchanan
White House
Communications
Director
McLean, VA

Joseph Coors
President
Adolph Coors Company
Golden, CO

Holly Coors
Chairwoman
Citizens for a New
Beginning
Golden, CO

Hon. Mike Curb
Lieutenant Governor
Sacramento, CA

Rich DeVos
President
Amway Corporation
Co-Chairman, Mutual
Broadcasting System
Ada, MI

John (Terry) Dolan
Chairman, National
Conservative PAC
Arlington, VA

Hon. John P. East
U.S. Senate
Washington, DC

Dr. Jerry Falwell
President
The Moral Majority
President, Liberty
Baptist College
Lynchburg, VA

Dr. Edwin J. Feulner
President
Heritage Foundation
Washington, DC

Hon. Jack Fields
U.S. Congress
Washington, DC

Frank Gannon
Vice President
The Viguerie Company
Falls Church, VA

Dr. Ronald S. Godwin
Vice President
The Moral Majority
Lynchburg, VA

Lt General Dan Graham
U.S. Army (Retired)
Chairman, The High
Frontier, Inc.
Washington, DC

J. Peter Grace
Chairman
W. R. Grace Co.
New York, NY

Hon. Jesse Helms
U.S. Senate
Washington, DC

Nelson Bunker Hunt
Chairman
Hunt Energy Corp.
Dallas, TX

Reed Irvine
President
Accuracy in Media
Washington, DC

Dr. Mildred Jefferson
Former President
National Right to
Life Committee
Boston, MA

Hon. Woody Jenkins
LA House of
Representatives
Baton Rouge, LA

Hon. Jack F. Kemp
U.S. Congress
Republican Conference
Washington, DC

Reed Larson
President, National
Right to Work Committee
Springfield, VA

Marvin Liebman
National Endowment
for the Arts
Washington, DC

James A. (Jim) Mather
Founder
Mr. Steak, Inc.
Denver, CO

Hon. Jim McClure
U.S. Senate
Washington, DC

F. Andrew Messing
Executive Director
The Conservative
Caucus, Inc.
Vienna, VA

Hon. Don Nickles
U.S. Senate
Washington, DC

Dr. Alton Ochsner, Jr
Physician
New Orleans, LA

Howard Phillips
National Chairman
The Conservative
Caucus
Vienna, VA

Dr. Pat Robertson
President, Christian
Broadcasting Network
Chancellor, CBN
University
Virginia, VA

James Robinson
Evangelistic Crusade
Fort Worth, TX

William A. Rusher
Publisher
National Review
New York, NY

William E. Saracino
Executive Director
Gun Owners of America
Sacramento, CA

Phyllis Schlafly
Syndicated Columnist
President
The Eagle Forum
Alton, IL

William Schneider, Jr.
Undersecretary of
State for Security
Assistance
Washington, DC

Dr. Cory SerVaas
Publisher
Saturday Evening Post
Indianapolis, IN

Frank Shakespeare
President, RKO General
Chairman, International
Communications Agency
New York, NY

Maj. General John K.
Singlaub
U.S. Army (Retired)
Tabernash, CO

Hon. Charles Stenholm
U.S. Congress
Coordinator,
Conservative Democratic
Forum
Washington, DC

Professor Lewis Tambs
National Security
Council
Washington, DC

Hon. Guy VanderJagt
U.S. Congress
Chairman, Republican
Congressional Committee
Washington, DC

Richard A. Viguerie
President
The Viguerie Company
Publisher
Conservative Digest
Falls Church,VA

Paul Weyrich
President
Free Congress Foundation
Washington, DC

James R. Whelan
Publisher
The Washington Times
Washington, DC

* 1982-83

zations, and right-wing religious leaders. CNP does not take public stands on policy issues but uses its vast influence network to effect policy changes. A key power base for the New Right, CNP draws its members from the Sunbelt states with 20 percent hailing from Texas. CNP serves as a fund-raising network for the FDN and General Singlaub. The Council invited Adolfo Calero of the FDN to speak to the group in January 1984, giving the contras valuable contacts among the New Right.

Free Congress Foundation
Washington, DC

Principals: Paul Weyrich (president), Charles Moser (secretary-treasurer), Kathleen Teague (chair), Senator William Armstrong (director).

In 1974, New Right activists Paul Weyrich and Joseph Coors created the Committee for the Survival of a Free Congress (CSFC) as a conservative political action committee. CSFC recently underwent a name change and is now the Free Congress Foundation. Like its predecessor, the Free Congress Foundation is dedicated to the election of conservative leaders to the U.S. House of Representatives and the Senate. The Free Congress Foundation provides financial assistance to candidates, offers tactical advice and services to candidates during the campaigns, and works with members of Congress on key legislative proposals. In its days as the CSFC, the group provided campaign funding to right-wing senators Jesse Helms and Orrin Hatch. It also trained over 7000 workers for Jerry Falwell's Moral Majority, Phyllis Schlafly's Eagle Forum, and various right-to-life and anti-union campaigns.

The Free Congress Foundation promotes the concept of anti-Soviet liberation movements and freedom fighters. In September 1982, Charles Moser formulated a plan to form a network of six national support committees for these movements in Afghanistan, Angola, Nicaragua, El Salvador, Kampuchea, and Vietnam. Members of the Nicaraguan committee included Dan Fefferman of the Freedom Leadership Foundation, Reed Irvine of the Council for the Defense of Freedom and Accuracy in Media, and L. Francis Bouchey of the Council for Inter-American Security. Members of the El Salvador committee included: Sam Dickens of New World Dynamic, Andy Messing of the National Defense Council, Reed Irvine, and Richard Araujo of the Heritage Foundation. Moser is the author of book published by the Free Congress Foundation entitled Combat on Communist Territory, which examines anticommunist insurgencies around the world and makes policy recommendations on U.S. support for those forces.

Freedom Research Foundation (FRF)

Principals: Jack Wheeler, Mike Kelly (Deputy Assistant Secretary for Manpower for the Air Force), Alex Alexiev (National Security Division of Rand Corporation).

FRF provides public relations and networking services for third-world anticommunist groups like the contras. For six months in 1983, Wheeler, self-described adventurer-philosopher, traveled with "anti-soviet liberation movements" in Nicaragua, Afghanistan and Angola as a guest of the right-wing Reason Foundation of Santa Barbara, California. Wheeler, who founded Freedom Research Foundation with the help of The Conservative Caucus, described his travel in front-page accounts in the Washington Times, owned by CAUSA.

Heritage Foundation
Washington, DC

Principals: Edwin J. Feulner, Jr. (president), William E. Simon (trustee), Joseph Coors (trustee), Lewis Lehrman (trustee), W. Bruce Weinrod, (Director of Foreign Policy and Defense Studies), J. Robert Fluor (trustee), Jack Wilson (trustee and Coor's personal aide), Frank Shakespeare, Richard Mellon Scaife.

This "aggressively conservative" think tank is another offspring of right-wing duo Joseph Coors and Paul Weyrich. Richard Mellon Scaife has been its principal funder. Funds for this New Right think tank also come from Dart Industries, Getty Oil, Bechtel, and the Readers Digest Association. Founded in 1973, the Heritage Foundation is a public policy research insti-

tute dedicated to free enterprise, anticommunism, limited government, and a strong
national defense. It publishes research
studies and policy analysis for the use of
government decision-makers and the public.
Roger Pearson, former president of the
World Anti-Communist League with a neo-Nazi
past, was a founding member of the foundation's journal Policy Review.

By some reports, the Foundation has become
the most influential of Washington policy
analysis organizations, pushing ahead of
the Brookings Institution and the American
Enterprise Institute. But its success
comes not from the quality of its research
and writing but from the marketing and
public relations skills of the Heritage
Foundation staff. According to its president, Edwin Feulner, the Heritage Foundation "has the intellectual resources necessary to change the course of history."
Feulner may be right. "Mandate for Leadership," a 1980 report published in time for
Ronald Reagan's election, made policy
recommendations for the new president.
According to a Heritage spokesperson, the
Reagan administration incorporated 65 percent of the document's proposals. Those
recommendations included unleashing the
CIA, using food as a weapon in the struggle
against communism, and overthrowing the
Sandinistas.

A Heritage Foundation Backgrounder written
by former CIA officer Cleto Di Giovanni has
been called "a virtual blueprint for U.S.
policy" in Nicaragua. Written in 1980, the
report suggested that the United States
carry out a "well orchestrated program
targeted against the Marxist Sandinista
government." Di Giovanni recommended U.S.
support of private sector groups in Nicaragua, including non-governmental labor
unions, the Church, "independent" political
parties, the "free press," and business.
Accusing the Sandinista government of de-
stabilizing activities in the region, Di
Giovanni asserted that "the security of El
Salvador requires the acceleration of the
removal of the government in Managua."

A 1985 Backgrounder by associate Virginia
Polk claimed that Guatemalan leaders had
"initiated significant political reforms to
propel their nation toward democracy."

Polk contended that the country no longer
had systematic labor repression and recommended U.S. support for the "civic action
programs" in the highlands. She referred
to the Guatemalan military's "model villages" as a "strategy for protecting the
Indian population in the war against Marxist guerrillas." Like Di Giovanni, Polk
proposed that private sector groups be
given increased U.S. assistance and suggested channeling anticommunist aid through
the Inter-American Foundation.

In its set of policy recommendations for
Reagan's second term, the Heritage Foundation called for the underwriting of paramilitary forces in nine countries that
"threaten United States interests."

**Institute on Religion and
Democracy (IRD)**
Washington, DC

Principals: Edmund W. Robb, (executive
officer).

Established in 1981, the IRD has 2000 members and is dedicated to "restoring democratic values" to churches. Its founders
included Penn Kemble, an initiator of the
Coalition for a Democratic Majority, and
Michael Novak, an associate of the American
Enterprise Institute and a director of the
Nicaraguan Freedom Fund. IRD tries to
identify the connections between religion
and the promotion of "democratic institutions" worldwide, and opposes churches
which support "leftist" groups. Described
by the Washington Post as an "upstart conservative faction bent on smearing its
opponents," the Institute gets most of its
funding from two right-wing foundations,
the Scaife Family Charitable Trusts and the
Smith Richardson Foundation. IRD bestows
an annual Religious Freedom Award and produces a bimonthly report, "Religion and
Democracy." It has also published two
reports on Central America: "Catholic
Church in El Salvador," and "Nicaragua: A
Revolution Against the Church?"

In 1983, the Institute led an attack
against the progressive National Council of
Churches for the council's approach to
and activities in Nicaragua, Cuba, and
Vietnam. In an article in Readers Digest

and an interview on the CBS news program "60 Minutes," IRD accused the NCC of anti-democratic actions. In another statement, executive officer Edmund Robb said the NCC had "substituted revolution for religion" and accused the group of "bias toward the totalitarian left."

In addition to money from right-wing foundations, the Institute has received funding from the U.S. Information Agency (USIA). The Nicaraguan government claims that the money is being funneled to dissidents in that country, and Foreign Minister Miguel d'Escoto has accused the IRD of being a CIA front, a charge which the Institute strongly denies. IRD has been a staunch supporter of Nicaragua's anti-Sandinista prelate, Cardinal Miguel Obando y Bravo.

Liberty Federation

Principals: Reverend Jerry Falwell.

The Liberty Federation, created in 1986, is Jerry Falwell's born again Moral Majority. Falwell and New Right tactician Paul Weyrich originally founded the Moral Majority as a grassroots social issue group of the religious right wing. It organized ministers to preach New Right politics and work for voter registration, operating under Falwell's dictum: "Get them saved, baptized and registered." In December 1984, Moral Majority, along with several other New Right groups, honored El Salvador's right-wing leader Roberto D'Aubuisson with a plaque thanking him for his "efforts for freedom."

In January 1986, the aggressively political Reverend Falwell announced the formation of the Liberty Federation which would have a broader outlook than Moral Majority. Falwell said that the Federation would take a more active role in certain debates, such as developing support for aid to the contras, while maintaining the older group's traditional concern for such issues as abortion and prayer in the schools.

National Strategy Information Center (NSIC)
New York, NY

Principals: Roy Godson (director, Georgetown University professor), Frank Barnett (president, Pentagon adviser, helped found the American Security Council, formerly worked with Smith Richardson Foundation), Joseph Coors, William Casey (past officer).

NSIC was founded in 1962 to "encourage civil-military partnership" for the purposes of informing the public so that they "maintain their core values of freedom and independence." Among its directors, officers, and advisers are such figures as Joseph Coors, Prescott S. Bush, and Frank Shakespeare (former USIA director, Heritage Foundation director). Numerous retired military commanders also direct NSIC including Admiral Elmo Zumwalt, who was the U.S. Naval commodore during the Vietnam war.

NSIC is a right-wing think tank for covert operations and military strategy. It works closely with the National Defense University and the National Security Studies Program at Georgetown University. NSIC is a principal advocate of low intensity conflict strategy, stressing the need for special operations, coordination with the private sector, and psychological operations. In the introduction to its 1984 book Special Operations in U.S. Strategy, the editors said that in the new ideological battlefield, "the problem begins at home" and called for psychological operations to prepare the U.S. public for low intensity conflict.

Western Goals Foundation (WGF)
Alexandria, VA

Principals: Linda Catoe Guell (president). Advisory Board: General John Singlaub, George S. Patton, Jr., Representatives Philip M. Crane, Bob Stump, and Bob Livingston, Senator Steve Symms, Admiral Thomas Moorer, Edward Teller ("father of the atomic bomb"), Sherman Unkefer, Dan Smoot.

Corporate Connections and Sponsors: Nelson Bunker Hunt, Roger Milliken (industrialist, union-buster, John Birch Society member), Deering-Milliken Corp, the Chance Foundation, the Grede Foundation, and the Ada Hearne Foundation (all three created by John Birch Society members), Springdale & Cherokee Mills, Deering-Milliken Research, and Knott's Berry Farm.

The Western Goals Foundation was founded in 1979 by the late Congressman Larry McDonald as a private intelligence gathering agency. McDonald, who was killed on the KAL-007 flight shot down by the Soviets in 1983, belonged to the John Birch Society and had ties to Chile's Augusto Pinochet. Other members of WGF have similar right-wing backgrounds. Former FBI man Dan Smoot, a current WGF board member, resigned from the Bureau in the 1950s to work for H.L. Hunt's political propaganda operation called Facts Forum. WGF member Hans Sennholz was a decorated pilot in Hitler's Luftwaffe. Sherman Unkefer, also a member of the John Birch Society, has served as an adviser to the Pinochet government, and reportedly worked with DINA, the CIA-supported Chilean security police agency.

Western Goals calls itself a "conservative, nonmembership, nonpartisan educational group." But its primary roles seem to be the collection and distribution of domestic intelligence and the coordination of conservative leadership in the United States. With its extensive computerized data on U.S. activists, WGF acts as a clearinghouse for police departments which have been barred from keeping political information on individuals not involved in crimes. Much of the information was compiled from U.S. government records which McDonald acquired as head of the House Un-American Activities Committee before it was disbanded. Other data were obtained from police department intelligence files in Los Angeles.

Central America's counterrevolutionary forces have also benefited from WGF's operations. Western Goals has advertised in the Washington Times and the newsletter of Council for Inter-American Security to raise money for the contras. WGF has sent "humanitarian relief supplies" such as clothing and medicines directly to the contras. Salvadoran rightist Roberto D'Aubuisson was honored at a dinner in 1984 which was co-sponsored by WGF.

Reference Notes

American Enterprise Institute (AEI)

NACLA Report on the Americas, July/August 1981; American Enterprise Institute Memorandum, Summer 1985; Leonard Silk and Mark Silk, The American Establishment (New York: Basic Books, Inc., 1980.

American Security Council

Alan Crawford, Thunder on the Right (New York: Pantheon Books, 1980); William W. Turner, Power on the Right (Berkeley: Ramparts Press, 1971); Kirkpatrick Sale, Power Shift: The Rise of the Southern Rim and Its Challenge to the Eastern Establishment (New York: Vintage Books, 1975); The Guardian, September 28, 1983; Village Voice, May 14, 1985; Council on Hemispheric Affairs, "Controversial Reagan Campaign Links with Guatemalan Government and Private Sector Leaders," October 30, 1980; Mother Jones, August/September, 1985; NACLA Report on the Americas, January/February, 1982; Covert Action Information Bulletin, Fall 1984.

Center for Strategic and International Studies (CSIS)

NACLA Report on the Americas, July/August 1981; Mother Jones, August/September 1985; Georges Fauriol and Eva Loser, "CSIS Latin American Election Studies Series--Guatemalan Election Study Reports," Background Study Report No.1, CSIS, 1985.

Committee for the Free World

Guardian, December 11, 1985; NACLA Report on the Americas, July/August 1981.

Committee on the Present Danger

Mother Jones, August/September 1985; Interview by Beth Sims with Richard Cady at University of New Mexico, February 28, 1986; Jerry Sanders, Peddlers of Crisis (South End: Boston, 1983).

The Conservative Caucus

Correspondence from Margie Wilkins, Director of Administrative Services, The Conservative Caucus, February 12, 1986; Alan Crawford, Thunder on the Right (New York: Pantheon Books, 1980); Covert Action Information Bulletin, Fall 1984; Washington Post, September 10, 1983; Encyclopedia of Associations, 1986; National Catholic Reporter, August 3, 1984; New York Times, July 15, 1984; TCC, "Ten Years of Progress."

Council for the Defense of Freedom

Encyclopedia of Associations, 1986; Phone interview by Deb Preusch with Don Irvine, February 13, 1986; Washington Inquirer, February 14, 1986; "The Washington Inquirer," Pamphlet by the Council for the Defense of Freedom, Washington, DC; "Accuracy in Academia," Pamphlet by the Council for the Defense of Freedom, Washington, DC; "Accuracy in Media," Pamphlet by the Council for the Defense of Freedom, Washington, DC; Accuracy in Media, AIM Report, February, 1986.

Council for Inter-American Security (CIS)

Covert Action Information Bulletin, Fall 1984; The Committee of Santa Fe, A New Inter-American Policy for the Eighties (Washington, DC: Council for Inter-American Security, Inc., 1980); Encyclopedia of Associations, 1986; Mother Jones, August/September 1985; Robert Emmet Moffit, "Soviet-American Relations in the 1980s--Taking 'Peaceful Coexistence' Seriously," in Robert W. Whitaker (ed.), The New Right Papers (New York: St. Martin's Press, 1982); Matthew Rothschild, "A Gala Occasion for the Contras," The Progressive, May 1985.

Council for National Policy

The Texas Observer, March 7, 1986; CNP letterhead and Officers List; Miami Herald, January 21, 1985; The Guardian, February 19, 1986; Cindy Buhl "Covert War: Private Aid to the Contras", no date.

Free Congress Foundation

Washington Post, December 5, 1984; Encyclopedia of Associations, 1986; Free Congress Foundation Brochure; Labor Report on Central America, September/October, 1985.

Freedom Research Foundation

Covert Action Information Bulletin, Fall 1984.

Heritage Foundation

Cleto Di Giovanni, Jr., "U.S. Policy and the Marxist Threat to Central America," in Peter Rosset and John Vandermeer, eds., The Nicaragua Reader: Documents of a Revolution Under Fire (New York: Grove Press, 1983) pp.190-191; Alan Crawford, Thunder on the Right (New York: Pantheon Books, 1980); Los Angeles Times, December 21, 1980; News Notes, Maryknoll Justice & Peace Office Newsletter, November 1985; New York Times, November 17, 1985; Mother Jones, August/September 1985; NACLA Report on the Americas, January/February 1982; Virginia Polk, "The New Guatemala Deserves U.S. Support," Heritage Foundation Backgrounder, May 22, 1985; Labor Report on Central America, September/October 1985; Washington Post, February 14, 1985.

Institute on Religion and Democracy (IRD)

Washington Post, March 19, 1983; Counterspy, June-August, 1983; Washington Post, February 27, 1983; "Nicaragua's State Security: Behind the Propaganda Mask," Interview with Alvaro Jose Baldizon Aviles, Briefing Paper by The Institute on Religion and Democracy, September 1985; Christian Century, January 22, 1986; Encyclopedia of Associations, 1986; NACLA Report on the Americas, July/August 1981.

Liberty Federation

Washington Post, December 5, 1984; NACLA Report on the Americas, July/August 1981.

National Strategy Information Center

Encyclopedia of Associations, 1986; Frank Barnett, B. Hugh Tovar, and Richard H. Shultz, eds., Special Operations in US Strategy (Washington: National Defense University Press,1984).

Western Goals Foundation

The National Reporter, Summer 1985; Encyclopedia of Associations, 1986; Washington Post, December 5, 1984; Common Cause Magazine, September/October, 1985.

Organization Links

	ACA	Ameri-cares	CBN	CAUSA	Dooley	FOA	IA	SMOM	NDCF	NFF	RRII	SOF	USCWF	WMR
ACA			X		X		X	X	X		X	X	X	X
Americares			X					X	X	X				
CBN	X	X				X	X	X	X		X			X
CAUSA										X	X			
Dooley	X					X		X						X
FOA			X		X			X						
IA	X		X											X
SMOM	X	X	X		X	X			X					
NDCF	X	X	X					X				X	X	X
NFF		X		X										
RRII	X		X	X								X		X
SOF	X								X		X			X
USCWF	X								X					
WMR	X		X		X		X		X			X	X	

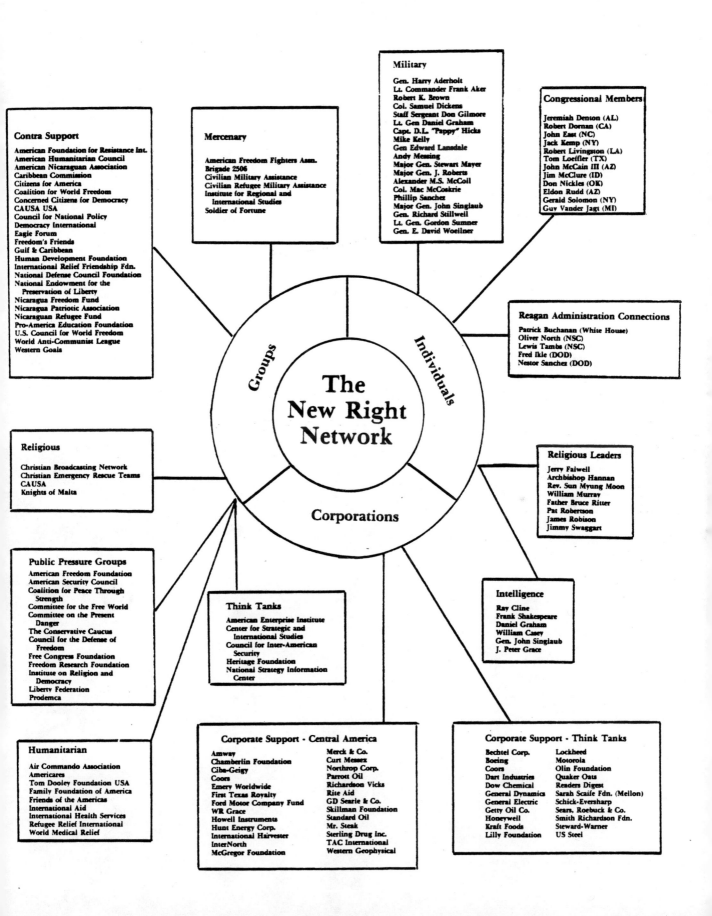

Military

Gen. Harry Aderholt
Lt. Commander Frank Aker
Robert K. Brown
Col. Samuel Dickens
Staff Sergeant Don Gilmore
Lt. Gen Daniel Graham
Capt. D.L. "Pappy" Hicks
Mike Kelly
Gen Edward Lansdale
Andy Messing
Major Gen. Stewart Mayer
Major Gen. J. Roberts
Alexander M.S. McColl
Col. Mac McCoskrie
Phillip Sanchez
Major Gen. John Singlaub
Gen. Richard Stillwell
Lt. Gen. Gordon Sumner
Gen. E. David Woellner

Congressional Members

Jeremiah Denton (AL)
Robert Dornan (CA)
John East (NC)
Jack Kemp (NY)
Robert Livingston (LA)
Tom Loeffler (TX)
John McCain III (AZ)
Jim McClure (ID)
Don Nickles (OK)
Eldon Rudd (AZ)
Gerald Solomon (NY)
Guy Vander Jagt (MI)

Contra Support

American Foundation for Resistance Int.
American Humanitarian Council
American Nicaraguan Association
Caribbean Commission
Citizens for America
Coalition for World Freedom
Concerned Citizens for Democracy
CAUSA USA
Council for National Policy
Democracy International
Eagle Forum
Freedom's Friends
Gulf & Caribbean
Human Development Foundation
International Relief Friendship Fdn.
National Defense Council Foundation
National Endowment for the
  Preservation of Liberty
Nicaragua Freedom Fund
Nicaragua Patriotic Association
Nicaraguan Refugee Fund
Pro-America Education Foundation
U.S. Council for World Freedom
World Anti-Communist League
Western Goals

Mercenary

American Freedom Fighters Assn.
Brigade 2506
Civilian Military Assistance
Civilian Refugee Military Assistance
Institute for Regional and
  International Studies
Soldier of Fortune

Reagan Administration Connections

Patrick Buchanan (White House)
Oliver North (NSC)
Lewis Tambs (NSC)
Fred Ikle (DOD)
Nestor Sanchez (DOD)

Groups

Individuals

The
New Right
Network

Corporations

Religious

Christian Broadcasting Network
Christian Emergency Rescue Teams
CAUSA
Knights of Malta

Religious Leaders

Jerry Falwell
Archbishop Hannan
Rev. Sun Myung Moon
William Murray
Father Bruce Ritter
Pat Robertson
James Robison
Jimmy Swaggart

Public Pressure Groups

American Freedom Foundation
American Security Council
Coalition for Peace Through
  Strength
Committee for the Free World
Committee on the Present
  Danger
The Conservative Caucus
Council for the Defense of
  Freedom
Free Congress Foundation
Freedom Research Foundation
Institute on Religion and
  Democracy
Liberty Federation
Prodemca

Think Tanks

American Enterprise Institute
Center for Strategic and
  International Studies
Council for Inter-American
  Security
Heritage Foundation
National Strategy Information
  Center

Intelligence

Ray Cline
Frank Shakespeare
Daniel Graham
William Casey
Gen. John Singlaub
J. Peter Grace

Humanitarian

Air Commando Association
Americares
Tom Dooley Foundation USA
Family Foundation of America
Friends of the Americas
International Aid
International Health Services
Refugee Relief International
World Medical Relief

Corporate Support - Central America

Amway	Merck & Co.
Chamberlin Foundation	Curt Messex
Ciba-Geigy	Northrop Corp.
Coors	Parrott Oil
Emery Worldwide	Richardson Vicks
First Texas Royalty	Rite Aid
Ford Motor Company Fund	GD Searle & Co.
WR Grace	Skillman Foundation
Howell Instruments	Standard Oil
Hunt Energy Corp.	Mr. Steak
International Harvester	Sterling Drug Inc.
InterNorth	TAC International
McGregor Foundation	Western Geophysical

Corporate Support - Think Tanks

Bechtel Corp.	Lockheed
Boeing	Motorola
Coors	Olin Foundation
Dart Industries	Quaker Oats
Dow Chemical	Readers Digest
General Dynamics	Sarah Scaife Fdn. (Mellon)
General Electric	Schick-Eversharp
Getty Oil Co.	Sears, Roebuck & Co.
Honeywell	Smith Richardson Fdn.
Kraft Foods	Steward-Warner
Lilly Foundation	US Steel

Part Four
New Right Humanitarians

Air Commando Association (ACA)
Fort Walton Beach, FL

Principals: Harry Aderholt (president),
Mac McCoskrie, Hap Lutz (vice president),
Will Elledge (treasurer), Charlie Hicks
(executive secretary).

ACA was formed in 1968 by Aderholt and
other members of the military's Air Commandos, which were at that time part of the
Special Operations Forces (SOF). Today,
its 1600 members are all former or current
SOF members. In its early days, ACA worked
almost exclusively in Southeast Asia. The
organization transported and distributed
supplies, donated primarily by World Medical Relief, to the CIA-organized Hmong army
and other anticommunist paramilitary groups
in Laos and Thailand.

Its current focus is Central America, where
it has worked with the armies in El Salvador and Guatemala and the contras in Honduras. Aderholt boasted that ACA worked
"hand in hand" with the U.S. Embassy and
MilGroup (military mission) in El Salvador.
ACA goods have been stored at both the
Ilopango Air Base near San Salvador and the
Knights of Malta warehouse inside the city.
Back in the United States, ACA has counted
on assistance from everybody from President
Reagan to various National Guard units to

facilitate the transport of its materials.
The August 1984 ACA newsletter reported
that the White House requested the Pentagon
DOD to have the Air Force fly its supplies
to El Salvador. One of ACA's fundraisers
is Captain Rip Kirby who is stationed at
Hurlburt Air Force Base, which is
frequently used by the CIA.

Since 1985 ACA has concentrated on expanding its program in the Highlands of Guatemala. In March 1985 ACA opened a clinic in
Nebaj in one of the military's civic action
zones which they call development poles.
Two other clinics, in Santa Cruz and Santa
Elena, have been opened more recently.
From March 1984 to October 1985, ACA and
the National Defense Council delivered more
than 10 million dollars worth in medical
supplies to development poles in Guatemala.

"We concentrate on Guatemala now because
the need is so critical," says Aderholt.
He calls ACA's work "civic action," noting
that the Air Commandos have always carried
out civic action programs ("we did it in
our spare time"). Another ACA member
described ACA's operations as "counterinsurgency civic action." As Aderholt
explains: "We're helping the refugees to
help them stay on our side. Anyone reading
anything sinister into this has got to be a
radical son-of-a-bitch."

ACA says it is "very, very pleased" with
the activities of the Guatemalan Army in
the Indian-populated Highlands. The Army
is also pleased with ACA's support and
provides its members with free transportation and room and board. Aviateca, the
Guatemalan airline controlled by the military, offers ACA free air transport for
supplies shipped from the United States.

In Nebaj, ACA volunteers are housed in the military outpost. Corporate contributors to ACA include Curt Messex and Northrop Corp.

American Foundation for Resistance International (RI)
New York, NY

Principals: Elizabeth Berns (executive director). Board Members: Albert Jolis, Vladimir Bukovsky, Jeane Kirkpatrick, Charles W. Sutherland, Yuri Yarim-Agaeve. Advisory Committee: William Buckley, Saul Bellow, Arnaud de Borchgrave, Midge Decter, Albert Shanker, Jack Wheeler.

Resistance International brings together traditional conservatives, neoconservatives, and New Rightists in support of so-called anti-Soviet liberation fighters. It sponsors publicity and fundraising tours for the contras.

American Freedom Fighters Association (AFFA)
Camden, TN

Principals: John Cattle (director).

AFFA supplies arms, ammunition, equipment and mercenaries to the contras. Cattle, who says he is working in Central America "to carry out God's will," explains that AFFA includes thousands of fundraisers and about 40 "hell raisers" who buy guns, munitions and equipment for the rebels and fight alongside them. The focus of AFFA is to strengthen the contras' southern front by laying the groundwork for communications and supply lines through Costa Rica. Cattle declares that he and other AFFA members are soldiers of God: "I have one job: to overthrow communism. As I see it, there are two armies—the Sandinista army and God's army. I'm in God's army. My job on this earth is to try to destroy the work of the devil."

Americares
New Canan, CT

Principals: Dr. Zbigniew Brzezinski (honorary chair and former National Security Adviser), Robert Macauley (president),

Father Bruce Ritter, Leila Macauley (secretary). Advisory Committee: J. Peter Grace (chair), Prescott Bush Jr. (Johnson & Higgins, brother of Vice President Bush), Sol M. Linowitz (Coudert Brothers), Frank Pace Jr. (International Executive Service Corps), Howard Rusk (Rusk Institution of Rehabilitation Medicine), William Simon (Citicorp, Nixon's Treasury Secretary), General Richard Stilwell.

Americares began its humanitarian work during the Vietnam war by forming "rescue missions" that helped Saigon children "raise money for their welfare by shining the shoes of American G.I.'s." It also helped with the 1975 evacuation airlift of Vietnamese associated with the U.S. occupation in Vietnam. The organization was formally incorporated in 1979, and in 1982 turned its attention to Poland. Immediately following the declaration of martial law in 1982, Americares shipped pharmaceutical supplies to the country for distribution by the Catholic Church. Supplied with more than a million pounds of chocolate by U.S. candy manufacturers, Americares has sponsored "Candylifts" to Polish children. The organization has also focused its humanitarian efforts on other political hot spots like Lebanon, Afghanistan, and Central America.

In Central America, Americares turns over most of its funds and donated materials to the Knights of Malta, which then distributes them in Central America. Because the Knights of Malta enjoy diplomatic privileges, Americares can ship supplies to Central America through diplomatic pouches that are not inspected by customs officials.

In 1983 Americares began its current focus on Central America relief efforts. Americares says that now "sea shipments to Central America leave on almost a weekly basis, filled with high priority medical supplies—all donated by American companies." In the last two years, Americares has sent 900,000 pounds valued at over $9.2 million in 22 sea shipments to El Salvador, 19 sea shipments of medical supplies valued at $7 million and 500,000 pounds of air cargo to Guatemala, and $3.2 million worth of shipments of medical and relief supplies to Honduras. Most of Americares' medical aid to Guatemala has been distributed through the armed forces as part of its resettlement program of model villages aimed at defeating leftist insurgents, said Roberto Alejos, co-chair of Knights of Malta in Honduras and Guatemala.

Pharmaceutical companies that have donated medical supplies to Americares include GD Searle & Co, Sterling Drug, Merck & Co, and Richardson Vicks. Macauley, a director of WR Grace, said his foundation has received donations from the top 40 U.S. medical corporations. In recent years, Americares has received as much as 10 percent of its funds from CBN. Americares was one of 19 recipients of the 1984 President's Volunteer Action Award for International Humanitarianism. Although Macauley claims that Americares has not shipped arms to the troublespots where it is involved, he said he would do so at the request of the U.S. government. "As a citizen," he said, "it is incumbent on me to carry out the orders of the commander-in-chief."

Brigade 2506
Miami, FL

Principals: Armando L. Calderin (secretary).

Founded in 1963, Brigade 2506 now has 1946 members in 11 states. Brigade members are mostly veterans of the CIA-sponsored Bay of Pigs invasion of Cuba in 1961, and its officials are prominent members of the Dade County Republican Party. The Brigade works closely with the CIA and U.S. landowners in Costa Rica.

U.S. mercenaries sent to Costa Rica have used the ranch of Bay of Pigs veteran John Hull as a base for raids inside Nicaragua. Steven Carr, one of five mercenaries arrested by the Costa Rican government in 1985, had been recruited by Brigade 2506. Before their arrest, the five mercenaries were in contact with John Hull, a U.S. millionaire who owns 6 ranches in Costa Rica and one in Florida. The arrested mercenaries said that several contra base camps were located on Hull's property and that military supplies were being transported from the Ilopango military air base in El Salvador to airstrips on the ranch. One of the arrested mercenaries claimed that Hull told him that he was receiving $10,000 per month from the National Security Council.

Bruce Jones, who owns a citrus farm in Costa Rica, also works with Brigade 2506. Life Magazine printed photographs of Jones training contras on his farm. Jones, an organizer of the Tucson chapter of the United States Council for World Freedom, admits that he has provided logistical support for the rebels, and the Life editor who worked on the story reported that Jones' CIA connection was confirmed by numerous sources in Costa Rica. The Brigade was reported to be involved in a 1985 plot to blow up the Cuban and Soviet embassies in Managua. Jesus Garcia, a participant in the failed plot, said he believed the plan had the backing of high officials of the U.S. government.

Caribbean Commission (CC)
New Orleans, LA

Principals: Dr. Alton Ochsner Jr., Archbishop Phillip Hannan (New Orleans), Louisiana State Representative Louis "Woody" Jenkins, Samuel Robinson (Robinson Lumber), Sergio Boltodano (executive director).

The Caribbean Commission, which was formed immediately after the Sandinista victory, raises funds for the contras among business owners in the southeastern states. It is closely linked to the FDN and regularly works with white supremacists. As with many other contra support groups, CC bases its counterrevolutionary thrust on religious principles. Organization founder

Ochsner sums up political developments in the Caribbean Basin this way: "It's God's forces versus anti-God forces." Ochsner's father, Alton Ochsner Sr., wrote the introduction to the white-supremacist book Dispossessed Majority. David Duke, a former KKK leader and founder of the National Association of White People, works closely with CC. The CC sent $500,000 worth of aid to the families of the contras along the Honduras-Nicaragua border in the 12 months ending July 1984. They also held a fundraiser for the FDN in September 1984. CC's latest program, "Adopt-a-Contra," allows individuals to "sponsor" a rebel and his family for so much money a month. Ochsner said "the whole purpose was to try and give [the contras] a good-guy image." In 1986 Ochsner provided free medical care to wounded contras at his clinic in New Orleans.

Baltodano says business owners should contribute to the CC to help maintain free enterprise in Central America. He suggests contributions may be easier from corporate units based outside the U.S.

Poster produced by the Caribbean Commission.

CAUSA USA (Confederation of the Associations for the Unification of the Societies of the Americas)
New York, NY

Principals: Phillip Sanchez (chair, former U.S. ambassador to Honduras), David Woellner (director), Daniel Graham, William Ley, Joseph Churba, Cleon Skousen (Mormon church leader), Lloyd Bucher (director), Colonel Bo Hi Pak (Moon's top deputy, chair of CAUSA International, and chair of News World Communications), Reverend Sun Myung Moon (founder; claims to be the true son of god), James Gavin (special assistant to Bo Hi Pak), Douglas MacArthur II (former ambassador to Japan, member of editorial advisory board of Washington Times), Larry R. Moffitt (executive director of World Media Association), Warren Richardson (former executive director of CAUSA, once served as general counsel to Liberty Lobby and as lobbyist for CALL—an anticommunist lobby), Joe Tully (director), John T. (Terry) Dolan (advisory board, chair of National Conservative Political Action Committee (NCPAC).

The Reverend Sun Myung Moon founded the Unification Church in 1954 in South Korea. He believes that the contest between God and Satan is carried out in international politics and economics. Moon says Satan uses trickery against God, and the church must also use trickery to advance its cause. This "heavenly deception," provides a religious justification for Moon to build his many front organizations. The church has branches in 130 nations. A 1978 Congressional Research Service report called the Unification Church "a tightly disciplined international political party" and found that it "resembles a multinational corporation, involving manufacturing, international trade, defense contracting, finance, and other business activities." Congress also found significant links between the Moonies and the South Korean CIA.

CAUSA was founded in 1980 as the political arm of the Unification Church in the western hemisphere. CAUSA (which means "cause" in Spanish) was later divided into two branch organizations: CAUSA International and CAUSA USA. CAUSA director Joe Tully says, "The cause is the defeat of communism." Other subsidiary organizations of the Unification Church with interest in Central America include: Washington Times, International Relief and Friendship Foundation, Nicaraguan Freedom Fund, Freedom

Leadership Foundation, and the Washington Institute for Values in Public Policy.

The Washington Times founded the Nicaraguan Freedom Fund to raise funds for the contras. International Relief and Friendship Foundation says its funds go to Nicaraguan refugees in Honduras and to pay the travel expenses of contra leaders. The Freedom Leadership Foundation has sponsored tours of Central America by right-wing legislators, and the Washington Institute for Values in Public Policy was set up as a way to integrate the traditional conservatives into church operations. The apparent purpose of these front organizations is to forge an alliance between the New Right and traditional conservatives and academics.

CAUSA's strategy bears strong resemblance to the operational principles of the new doctrine of low intensity conflict (LIC) that is fast gaining popularity in the Pentagon. LIC doctrine calls for close coordination of psychological, political, economic, and military operations to fight back against the perceived communist advance. Bo Hi Pak, Moon's top deputy and a former South Korean military attache, described the church's strategy this way: "It's a total war, basically a war of ideas. A war of minds. The battlefield of the human mind. So in this war, the entire things [sic] will be mobilized: political means, social means, economical means, and propagandistic means. Basically trying to take over the other person's mind. That is what the Third World War is all about. The war of ideology." Bo Hi Pak has acknowledged receiving CIA funds.

CAUSA sponsors anticommunist conferences in Central America. At one such conference in San Pedro Sula, Honduras, CAUSA flew in L. Francis Bouchey of the Council on Inter-American Security to address the participants. CAUSA maintains several offices in Central America and is currently trying to forge anticommunist coalitions throughout the region.

The FDN's Fernando Chamorro said that CAUSA representatives were working with anti-Sandinista forces as early as 1981 and paid for his travel that year to the United States to unify Somocista elements. Jon Lee Anderson, an associate of Jack Anderson, reported that CAUSA airlifted supplies to the contras immediately after Congress first cut off aid. Contra leaders told Jon Lee Anderson that CAUSA and Friends of the Americas were two of the main "sources of supplies and cash for their families." Investments in banks, arms sales, industry, and real estate finance CAUSA activities. Bankers in Uruguay, where the church has considerable financial investments, say that Reverend Moon uses his profits to directly fund the contras.

Christian Broadcasting Network (CBN)
Virginia Beach, VA

Principals: M.G. "Pat" Robertson.

Ex-golden gloves champion, ex-marine, and former corporate official of WR Grace in Central America, Robertson founded CBN in 1959. Robertson, the son of former U.S. Senator A. Willis Robertson (D-VA), has been very successful in creating a high-tech ministry, including a viewer-supported talk show, "The 700 Club" which reaches 30 million homes. CBN is a communications conglomerate with the third largest cable network, three television stations in the United States and one in Lebanon, a radio station, and a communications satellite. It also has a book-publishing corporation, a university, and a humanitarian organization called Operation Blessing which distributed $50 million in aid in 1984. Its annual revenues of $240 million a year require a minimal amount of financial disclosure.

To help him in his current presidential campaign, Robertson set up the Freedom Council, a political network with volunteer lobbyists in every state, purchased a 24 seat jet and set up a think-tank called the National Perspectives Institute.

In June 1985, the Miami Herald reported that CBN is considered the largest private donor to the contras. CBN has worked with the following groups to provide aid to Central America: Air Commandos Association, World Medical Relief, International Aid, Americares, National Defense Council, Dooley Foundation, Friends of the Americas, and Knights of Malta. Operation Blessing also has given $3 million to the Nicaraguan Patriotic Association (NPA), a FDN contra organization.

The Air Commandos say that Captain Robert Warren (ret.), who is in charge of Operation Blessing, approached them in August 1984 to begin joint medical efforts in the Guatemalan Highlands. In 1985, ACA reported the beginning of a new project ("in cooperation with the government of Guatemala") with CBN, National Defense Council, and World Medical Relief to send medical personnel to treat Indians. In El Salvador, CBN has worked with the U.S. MilGroup, Knights of Malta, World Medical Relief, and Refugee Relief International as part of the military civic action program.

The 700 Club, which collects $15 a month from each of its members, promotes the humanitarian work of the Friends of the Americas (FOA). FOA's Diane Jenkins has appeared on CBN to solicit funds. Other guests of The 700 Club talk program include Steadman Fagoth of MISURA, Adolfo Calero of FDN, and former Guatemalan president Rios Montt.

CBN has counted on the U.S. military to get some of its humanitarian assistance to Central America. Some transportation is supplied by Operation Handclasp, a U.S. Navy program that ships donated goods to ports of call around the world. Transportation has also been provided by the Air Force. CBN supplies have been stored with DOD approval at Fort Meade in Maryland and the Selfridge Air Base in Michigan prior to shipment to Central America. Robertson has traveled to Honduras and given religious services in several camps of contras, and he says that CBN supplies "chaplaincy services and Bibles to the contras."

Citizens for America (CFA)

Principals: Lewis Lehrman (owner of Rite Aid drug store, Heritage Foundation trustee, friend of Reagan), Joseph and Holly Coors, Nelson Bunker Hunt, T. Boone Pickens, Holmes Tuttle, Earle Jorgensen (friends of Reagan and members of his "kitchen cabinet").

Citizens for America was established in 1983 with $1 million in "seed money" from wealthy supporters including Joseph Coors and the "blessing of Reagan and his closest aides." CFA devoted major efforts to winning congressional support for the contras--they brought 20 contras to the U.S. to campaign in 200 congressional districts for resumption of contra aid. CFA was responsible for the June 2, 1985 meeting between A. Calero (FDN), J. Savimbi (UNITA), and leaders of CIA-backed forces in Afghanistan and Laos, which resulted in the founding of Democracy International.

Civilian Materiel Assistance (CMA)
Memphis, TN

Principals: Tom Posey (president), Jim Turney (national director).

According to Tom Posey, a former Marine corporal, CMA began in July 1983 when he and several other veterans decided to help the anticommunist forces in Central America. He says that General Gustavo Alvarez Martinez, then commander of the Honduran military, invited his group to Honduras and that the U.S. embassy arranged the first contacts between CMA and the Honduran Army. Since then, CMA, known initially as Civilian Military Assistance, has taken over many of the functions previously performed for the contras by the CIA, including providing trainers, advisers, and maintaining a logistic pipeline.

After two of its members were shot down in Nicaragua in September 1984 while flying in a CIA helicopter, CMA chapters have sprung up across the country. CMA now claims chapters in all 50 states and 7 foriegn countries, with a membership of 5000. Members of CMA are recruited through National Guard contacts, at gun shows, and in gun shops. The Alabama National Guard Special Forces, which specializes in counterinsurgency, is an especially fruitful source of new CMA members, but Posey says 50 percent of CMA's members are military veterans. In 1984 Staff Sergeant Don Gilmore founded an offshoot of CMA, Civilian Refugee Military Assistance, in Memphis.

Captain D.L. (Pappy) Hicks (president of the Texas chapter of CMA) is proud of the help CMA has given to Nicaraguan contras and their families living in the Atlantic Coast region. "I kill people for what I think is an ideology and for a religious purpose," says Captain Hicks, "I don't want nobody impressing their way of life and their political beliefs and their religious beliefs upon me. So I don't think it's heathenistic or barbaric that people like me do what we're doing. I'll do it as long as communism exists or I die." CMA members have acknowledged that CMA operates a commando school and has launched several "training missions" into Nicaragua. The motto of the FDN contras, "With God and Patriotism, we will defeat Communism," is repeatedly quoted in the group's brochure, which asks those interested in training anticommunists in a foreign country to send the organization their resumes.

In El Salvador, the U.S. MilGroup has arranged contacts between CMA and the Salvadoran Army's chief of staff and CMA has supplied the Salvadoran military with training and supplies. U.S. Army Major Charles McAnarney, a logistics officer stationed at the U.S. embassy in San Salvador, helped process 11 shipments of military supplies from CMA to the Salvadoran Army between November 1983 and March 1984.

Adolfo Calero, FDN's commander-in-chief, declared once that "The FDN and the CMA are one!" CMA helps train the contras and has even offered to send the contras a combat-ready George Patton Brigade made up of 3,000 American volunteers. "We teach them the basics—booby traps, zipguns, basic survival skills, that sort of thing," said one CMA member. FDN leader Calero said CMA bought a cargo plane in the U.S. to transport private aid. In 1985, CMA said it provided over $3 million worth of non-lethal supplies and 15,000 man-hours of military training to the contras. Calero says CMA has trained FDN in the use of air-to-surface missiles, but Posey denies this. CMA has vowed to double its 1985 contribution in 1986. CMA also intends to raise enough money through donations to purchase four Medevac helicopters for the FDN. In early 1985 CMA members spent six weeks in Rus Rus, Honduras training guerrillas who later went on a mission to destroy a bridge in Nicaragua.

Coalition for World Freedom (CWF)

Founded in 1985 by John Singlaub, the Coalition for World Freedom and the United States Covenant for World Freedom (USCWF) is made of 17 groups including CMA, Military Magazine, American Freedom Co., Christian Mandate for America, Voice of Americanism, Society of Vietnamese Rangers, The Conservative Caucus, American Security Council, Fund for American Majority, and Ukrainian Congressional Committee of America. The Coalition is a "nationwide network for Anti-Communist groups" formed "to disseminate information and counteract disinformation." USCWF says that member groups will maintain their own identity but "in the area of Anti-Communism, they function as a member of a network."

Concerned Citizens for Democracy (CCD)
Miami, FL

Principals: Carlos Perez.

CCD is an organization of Cuban-American business owners who are members of the Cuban Republican Club of Miami. Perez, the organization's founder and chair, also chaired Viva '84, the Hispanic arm of the Reagan-Bush fund-raising campaign. President Reagan often uses the example of Perez, a Cuban exile and a successful banana importer, as an exile success story. The group's main project was a recent trip to Washington of 150 mostly Cuban-Americans and Nicaraguan businessmen to lobby for congressional aid to the contras. Receiving tax-exempt status in March 1985, the CCD had a testimonial dinner in June 1985—half the proceeds were promised to foundations which feed and shelter Nicaraguan refugees and the other half to CCD.

Democracy International (DI)
Washington, DC

Principals: Lew Lehrman (owner of Rite Aid drug stores).

The organization was founded in June 1985 following a unity meeting of freedom fighters sponsored by Citizens for America.   It helped form a coalition of anticommunist guerrillas from Afghanistan, Nicaragua, Laos, and Angola, and its office serves as a central clearing house for these guerrilla movements.

Tom A. Dooley Foundation/InterMed USA
New York, NY

Principals: Verre Chaney.

The Dooley Foundation, founded in 1961, gives to the FDN in Honduras and to El Salvador. It sends medical supplies from World Medical Relief directly to the FDN and indirectly through Air Commandos and Friends of the Americas.

Tom Dooley was the famous jungle doctor of Laos whose clinics provided cover for intelligence activities. Dooley's clinics were established near the Chinese border at a time when the CIA was launching cross-border operations in southern China. Dooley gave the CIA intelligence reports on the area. Working with Dooley were U.S. Special Forces medics, posing as civilians. Navy doctor Dooley worked for an operation identified by the Pentagon Papers as being part of a CIA effort headed by Colonel Edward Lansdale to bolster pro-U.S. elements and destabilize the 1954 Indochina agreement. Dooley died in 1961.

Eagle Forum
Alton, IL

Principals: Phyllis Schlafly.

The Forum's primary function is to lobby against the ERA, but its 50,000 members also find time to assemble toilet kits for the contras. The Dallas chapter collected articles for 300 toilet kits for individual contra fighters. According to Elaine Middendorf, the Missouri state director, "The Russians are probably supplying the Sandinistas with even better kits. Then again, maybe the Russians don't have the little necessities of life that are really minor in America....There's a toothbrush and toothpaste—Crest, Colgate....There's aspirin. Bayer and Anacin. Insect repellent, water purification tablets, Life Savers, Doublemint Gum—I guess to 'double your fight'—shaving cream and disposable razors, and an aluminum mirror that you can prop up and shave with....It's part of man's dignity to be able to keep some semblance of being civilized in battle. And there's foot powder. When their feetsies in their bootsies start hurting, I guess it does give them some relief." The kits were shipped to the contras by USCWF in Phoenix.

Family Foundation of America (FFA)
Edgewater, FL

Principals: Kenneth Wells.

Kenneth Wells founded FFA in 1984. He is also the co-founder of the Freedoms Foundation in Valley Forge and is an honorary lifetime member of the Knights of Malta. Wells has also been commended by the right-wing Norman Vincent Peale Foundation. FFA's goods have gone to Honduras, El Salvador, Guatemala, and Costa Rica. Since 1985 Wells has concentrated on El Salvador where he distributes donated supplies through the army's civic action program.

The U.S. MilGroup in San Salvador says that FFA supplies are an essential part of the army's civic action program. Wells packs the clothing, medicine, garden seeds, and food donations in barrels in which he also places a U.S. flag, "It offers the only thing they can pray for."

Bob Heintzelman, who works with Wells, sends soccer balls to El Salvador for distribution by the army's civic action and psychological operations teams. "The rebels have been blowing up or burning up every bit of athletic equipment," says Heintzelman. "They come in and shoot a few old men, rape the girls and then destroy the athletic equipment." When asked why he coordinates his humanitarian efforts with the military, Wells replied: "This is my goal to make armies of this area serve the people. The day of the death squad is gone. A new method of war is developing: 1) brilliantly trained soldiers, not only in weaponry, but in service to the people; 2) flooding of civic action provided by people who have surpluses; 3) trained people in villages capable of defending villages, not a part of the army."

Freedom's Friends (FF)
Murray Faith Ministries
Coppell, TX

Principals: William Murray.

William Murray, son of the well-known atheist Madalyn Murray O'Hair, is a fundamentalist minister who says he has renounced his "Marxist-Leninist upbringing." He now pursues anticommunist politics with the unique energy of a recent convert. FF stockpiles relief supplies in a warehouse in Addison, Texas. Murray was working on refugee aid projects through Murray Faith Ministries before he launched FF as a separate project in July 1985. Murray says the aid is directed to those refugees with FDN connections.

Friends of the Americas (FOA)
Baton Rouge, LA

Principals: Louisiana State Representative Louis "Woody" and Diane Jenkins.

Since its founding in 1984 by the Jenkins husband and wife team, FOA has become a major relief organization in Central America. Its operations are spread up and down the isthmus but concentrated mostly along the Honduras-Nicaragua border. In 1985, FOA also provided relief supplies to Mexican earthquake victims.

Its projects in Honduras are located in the two major areas where contras have their base camps. In the La Mosquitia area, where it counts on the assistance of AID, FOA has constructed a landing strip, refugee center, hospital, five nutrition centers, and several schools. FOA provides food, clothing, and medical assistance to the contras and their families in the towns of Rus Rus, Awasbila, Uscan, and Alatiz, villages which are near MISURA camps and are located within miles of the Nicaragua border. MISURA leader Steadman Fagoth in 1984 said that FOA assistance allowed his men "to concentrate on the war" instead of having to worry about their families' welfare.

FOA also serves the Nicaraguan contra population in the border area around Danli, the center of the FDN contras. FOA says that its clinics in Cifuentes and Las Trojes are "within feet of the border", and that the Las Trojes "position has been shelled by Sandinista mortars."

FOA claims that it targets the border region of Honduras only because it wants to assist the refugees there. Carmen Winkler,

FOA's Honduran director said, "We don't help freedom fighters....I help the families." But she acknowledges that, "All the people there [in La Mosquitia] are the families of the freedom fighters."

FOA spearheads the national "Shoe Boxes for Liberty" campaign that has distributed over 20,000 small boxes of personal supplies for Nicaraguan refugees. A label on the shoe boxes makes FOA's political orientation obvious: "We hope the small things in this box are useful in your struggle for liberty." FOA relief supplies are transported to Central America by DOD under the space-available provisions of the Denton Amendment. But even before Congress authorized the Pentagon to use its planes to transport private supplies, FOA shoe boxes and other supplies were being carried to Honduras by Air National Guard units in Mississippi and Louisiana.

Within Honduras, FOA uses Wings of Hope and a CIA-created airline called SETCO to transport its supplies. In the capital city of Tegucigalpa, FOA has stored materials at the FDN safehouse. FOA's liaison with the Honduran army, Captain Lionel Luque Jimenez, doubles as the army's liaison with the FDN. FOA's Fall 1984 "Friends Report" asked contributors for a large airplane, 4-wheel drive vehicles, pick-up trucks, generators, walkie-talkies, boats, outboard motors, short-wave radios, and battery-operated radios.

In January 1986, Woody Jenkins, who has served as Secretary of the Conservative Caucus, and executive director of the Council for National Policy, said that FOA planned to open clinics in Costa Rica, Guatemala, and El Salvador within the year. As in Honduras, the Costa Rican clinic will serve only Nicaraguan refugees. The organization's new board of directors in Guatemala includes the part-owner of the right-wing La Prensa Libre daily newspaper, Harris Whitbeck (a former close adviser of President Efrain Montt and current director of an AID-funded relief organization known as PAVA), and Jorge Serrano (a right-wing evangelist who recently ran for president). The Guatemalan FOA plans to operate a mobile clinic in the development poles of the Highlands. In El Salvador, FOA has announced plans to set up a clinic to treat displaced people—a project that will be part of AID's extensive pacification program for that country.

President Reagan has personally commended FOA's work for the freedom fighters. In April 1985, Reagan awarded Diane Jenkins the First Annual Ronald Reagan Humanitarian Award at the Nicaraguan Refugee Fund dinner in Washington.

Gulf and Caribbean (G&C)
Washington, DC

Principals: Dan Kuykendall.

"My membership looks like a Who's Who of Texas" said Dan Kuykendall, former member of Congress from Tennessee who runs G&C. "But they aren't part of this straight-aid-to-the-contra. They don't like to be a part of anything that appears radical." His group's main activity has been to sponsor "outstanding scholars" who are "really credible." Kuykendall boasts that one of the accomplishments of the group was the introduction of the term "democratic revolution" used for the contra force. "That came from a booklet we published, I remember the time I showed that [term] to someone at the White House. He said, 'Is that us?'." Kuykendall said the group has sponsored many trips to Central America and helped place articles in major U.S. dailies.

Institute for Regional and International Studies (IRIS)
Boulder, CO

Principals: John Singlaub, Alexander M.S. McColl (director), Robert Brown, William Guthrie, Tom Reisinger.

Founded by Singlaub, and headed by McColl, this private training organization was established to provide intelligence and psychological warfare training to the Salvadoran armed forces and the contras.

International Aid (IA)
Spring Lake, MI

Principals: Dr. James E. Franks Sr., and James E. Franks Jr.

International Aid describes itself as an "independent, non-profit, inter-denominational relief and mission service organization." It has worked with World Medical Relief, Air Commandos, and Christian Broadcasting Network to get supplies to Guatemala and Honduras since 1984.

International Relief Friendship Foundation (IRFF)

IRFF started in 1976 with a $225,000 grant from the Unification Church, and about 90 percent of its annual budget (under $200,000) still comes from the Church. IRFF's aid is distributed to "recently arrived refugees" along the Nicaragua border. In 1984, IRFF sent 1000 pounds of clothing, and nearly 7 tons of food and medical supplies to Miskito refugees in Honduras.

Knights of Malta (SMOM)
East Canton, OH

Principals: J. Peter Grace (chair of U.S. chapter), William Simon, Prescott Bush Jr., William Casey (CIA director) Alexander Haig (former Secretary of State), Senator Jeremiah Denton, Senator Pete Domenici, Lee Iacocca (Chrysler), Barron Hilton (Hilton Hotels), Lt. Gen. Rinehart Gehlan (a Nazi Intelligence and Covert Operations officer who was recruited by the CIA), William F. Buckley, William P. Clark (former National Security Adviser), and Frank Shakespeare (former director of the U.S. Information Agency and a director of the Heritage Foundation).

This elite Catholic organization models itself after an order of soldier-monks that fought in the Crusades. Its formal name is the Sovereign Military Hospitaller Order of St. John, of Jerusalem, of Rhodes, and of Malta. SMOM, which has 10,000 members in 42 countries, is organized diplomatically as being part of the State of the Vatican. Its unusual status of a sovereign nation without its own territory allows the organization to send items across borders via "diplomatic pouch," meaning that they are not subject to review by local customs authorities.

Social historian Stephen Birmingham said, "The Knights of Malta comprise what is perhaps the most exclusive club on earth. They are more than just Catholic aristocracy. They can pick up a telephone and chat with the Pope." The U.S. chapter has 1,750 members and has been called "the cutting edge of right-wing Catholicism, a hidden mating ground where the Catholic church and the U.S. ruling elite intersect." During the Vietnam war, SMOM showed strong support for U.S. military intervention in Southeast Asia and contributed to the U.S. government's pacification campaign in South Vietnam. At least eight knights are directors of WR Grace, and J. Peter Grace directs the U.S. branch of SMOM.

In the last few years, U.S. knights have shown increasing interest in Central America and currently distribute humanitarian assistance through military civic action programs in Honduras, Guatemala, and El Salvador as well as to the Nicaraguan contras.

SMOM's work in Central America pushed forward in 1983 after J. Peter Grace worked out an agreement between Americares and SMOM to ship and distribute medical supplies to the region. In 1983-84 $14 million of Americares donations were channeled through the Knights: $10 million to El Salvador, $680,000 to Miskito Indians in Honduras, and $3.4 million to Guatemala.

Local knights in Central America generally handle the distribution of the supplies and arrange contacts with the local armed forces. Like their counterparts in the

United States, the knights in Central America come from the upper crust and espouse right-wing politics. In El Salvador, local SMOM members are well-to-do businessmen, lawyers, doctors or others who often have facilities such as warehouses, trucks or planes at their disposal.

Heading El Salvador's SMOM are Gerald Coughlin (retired FBI agent and current executive of International Harvester—Americares uses International Harvester's warehouse in San Salvador to store its donations) and Miguel Salaverria (manager of the Prieto coffee export company). Salaverria said there are about 20 Salvadoran knights but only 5 or 6 remain in the country. Besides Americares, SMOM in El Salvador works with such charitable organizations as the Tom Dooley Foundation, Project Hope, and the right-wing Salvadoran-American Foundation. It helps supply the military's resettlement center and has set up an orphanage, health center, and hospitals as part of the military's pacification program. It also runs a food distribution program in the country.

Salaverria says the U.S. embassy "is very helpful" in arranging transport into El Salvador, while the Salvadoran armed forces help move SMOM supplies. SMOM's leading knight in Honduras and Guatemala is Roberto Alejos, the Guatemalan oligarch whose plantation was used by the CIA to train Cuban exiles for the Bay of Pigs invasion of Cuba in 1961. Alejos says that most of the goods distributed by SMOM and Americares in Guatemala in 1984 went to the military's model village and development poles.

Asked why SMOM does not rely on more established groups to deliver their aid, Grace said that, "The knights have been doing this for 900 years. They have their own cross [the Maltese cross]. They consider themselves way beyond the Red Cross."

National Defense Council Foundation (NDCF)
Alexandria, VA

Principals: Andy Messing, Edward Lansdale, John Singlaub, Harry Aderholt.
Founded in 1978 by Andy Messing, NDCF's focus is on supplying medical supplies to the Guatemalan development poles. NDCF's efforts in Guatemala were first suggested to Guatemala's president, General Mejia Victores, in 1984 by Gabriel Gomez del Rio (the executive director of Latin America affairs for NDCF, former AID employee in Guatemala, and former Cuban "freedom fighter"). NDCF works closely with ACA in Guatemala. Supplies donated to NDCF are distributed by ACA and the Guatemalan Army in the militarized development poles. In 1985, NDCF delivered one shipment of over 20 tons of medical supplies for the military's Operation Child civic action program for distribution to Indians in the Highlands. With an annual budget of $250,000 NDCF also organizes fact-finding tours to Central America for members of Congress.

National Endowment for the Preservation of Liberty (NEPL)
Washington, DC

Principal: Spitz Channell.

Channell founded NEPL in 1984, and it is now called the fastest growing non-profit organization in Washington. Channell has previously been a principal figure in the National Conservative Political Action Committee and the American Conservative Trust (which spent a half million dollars in a 1983 advertising and information campaign to "inform the American people on the crisis in Nicaragua and the need to support Reagan's policy").

NEPL in early 1986 hired the public relations firm International Business Communications, run by former CIA and State Department officials, to coordinate a publicity tour for a Nicaraguan contra. In March 1986, NEPL spent a small fortune on

TV ads supporting aid to the contras. The ads claimed that Libya supplies Nicaragua with terrorist experts. NEPL has also produced two 30-minute films on the purported Sandinista threat.

Nicaraguan Development Council
Washington, DC

Principals: Bosco Matamoras.
This tax-exempt corporate arm of the FDN was founded in 1984 and focuses on fundraising. The organization was established by associates of the Barnett & Alagia law firm. The same firm helped incorporate two related organizations, the Human Development Fund and Nicaragua Refugee Fund. Barnett & Alagia also set up the Cuban-American National Foundation, the Salvadoran-American Foundation (which works with the Knights of Malta and the Air Commandos) and the Guatemala Freedom Foundation, organizations that appear to be CIA-initiated. Edgar Chamorro, a former FDN leader, said that the CIA founded HDF to divert attention away from its attempt to launder funds for the contras through foreign governments.

Nicaraguan Freedom Fund (NFF)
Washington, DC

Principals: Jeane Kirkpatrick, William Simon (chair, former Secretary of Treasury under Nixon), Midge Decter (Committee for a Free World), Michael Novak (American Enterprise Institute scholar and syndicated columnist), Charlton Heston, W. Clement Stone.

NFF was founded in 1985 by the Washington Times, a Washington daily owned by the Unification Church, to raise funds for the contras. "Unlike other papers," said editor Arnaud de Borchgrave, "we are willing to put our money where our opinions are." Colonel Bo Hi Pak, top deputy to Reverend Sun Myung Moon, immediately pledged $100,000 to the fund drive. Named to head the new organization were William Simon and Michael Novak. Simon and Novak are both board members of PRODEMCA, a private group which channels U.S. government funds to the anti-Sandinista political opposition.

Kirkpatrick, a NFF board member, initially pledged $20,000 to the contra support effort. Later, she requested that Ralston Purina give NFF the $2,500 she had earned for allowing the company to photograph her Siamese cat, Arthur. In NFF's first six months, NFF's executive director Hal Eberle reported that in its first several months NFF had raised $350,000, which was turned over to Americares. The Times campaign was welcomed by FDN spokesperson Bosco Matamoras, who said the money for food and clothing would free up funds which the group can use "for other supplies."

Nicaragua Refugee Fund
Washington, DC

Principals: True Davis (chair, former ambassador to Switzerland, former Assistant Secretary of Treasury, former executive director of Inter-American Development Bank), Woody Jenkins, Dr. Alvaro Rizo Castellon (former career diplomat for the Somoza government), Joseph C. Luman (former State Department Foreign Service Officer in Vietnam), Dr. Luis E. Aguilar (professor at Georgetown University, consultant to National Endowment for Democracy).

The NRF was founded in September 1984 following a fund-raising effort organized by the FDN through a Panamanian corporation called the Human Development Foundation that it established with the assistance of the CIA. An agreement between the Miner and Fraser Public Affairs Inc. and the Nicaraguan Development Council (the FDN's corporate arm) created NRF. Alavaro Rizo, who was working for the firm at the time, arranged the deal.

The organization is best known for the extravagant $250-a-head fundraising dinner it sponsored in April 1985. Corporations represented at the NRF dinner through top executives included: WR Grace, Adolph Coors, InterNorth, Standard Oil, Hunt Oil, and Western Geophysical. Working on the Dinner Committee were James Lyon, Ellen St. John Garwood, Nelson Bunker Hunt, Roger Staubach, Harry Lucas Jr., and Spitz Channell. President Reagan told the freedom diners: "While the world was turning away, you were helping. People like you are America at its best." The dinner raised a total of $219,525, but Nicaraguan anticommunist refugees received only $3,000 after deducting expenses of $218,376. A consultant payment of $50,000 went to Miner and Fraser Public Affairs.

Pro-America Educational Foundation (PAEF)
Washington, DC

Principals: Joan L. Hueter.

With the approval of DOD, PAEF used military bases at Fort Meade, Maryland and Selfridge, Michigan to store supplies they collected in spring 1984. In May 1984 the Air Force flew the supplies from both bases to Central America free of charge. PAEF has raised a total of $6.3 million from conservative political groups for Central America; $1 million in medical supplies contributed by major pharmaceutical companies went specifically to Nicaraguan refugees in Honduras.

PRODEMCA (Friends of the Democratic Center in Central America)

Principals: R. Penn Kemble (Institute of Religion and Democracy), William Doherty (American Institute for Free Labor Development), Jeane Kirkpatrick, J. Peter Grace, Jorge Mas Canosa (Cuban American Foundation), Max Singer (Potomac Organization), Angier Biddle Duke (former U.S. Ambassador to El Salvador), Michael Novak, Ben Wattenberg (Coalition for a Democratic Majority), and William Simon.

Founded in 1981 with grants from the right-wing Smith-Richardson, Olin, and Carthage foundations, PRODEMCA receives much of its funding from the National Endowment for Democracy (NED), an organization founded by the Reagan administration to promote democracy and free enterprise in the third world. PRODEMCA, initially known as the Citizens' Committee for the Pro-Democratic Forces in Central America, acts as a channel for NED funds to the anti-Sandinista opposition. Describing the FDN as a "democratic alternative," PRODEMCA has run full-page ads in the New York Times and Washington Post supporting aid to the contras. PRODEMCA has hosted press conferences for the FDN and gave $100,000 in NED funds to the anti-Sandinista newspaper La Prensa. With a $200,000 grant from NED, PRODEMCA created the Nicaraguan Center for Democratic Studies, the U.S. office of the arch-conservative political coalition headed by Arturo Cruz. It used the rest of the grant to fund the Permanent Commission of Human Rights in Nicaragua, the main source of charges of human rights abuses by the Sandinistas.

Refugee Relief International Inc. (RRII)
Lafayette, CO

Principals: Thomas Reisinger (president), John Singlaub, Harry Aderholt, Alexander M.S. McColl.

Set up with the help of the Omega Group (See SOF) in 1982, RRII provides medical training and supplies to El Salvador and to the contras. RRII says it is dedicated "to help the sick and those wounded by communist supported guerrillas." Through an agreement with Air Commandos, RRII distributes World Medical Relief supplies in El Salvador. RRII paramedics and doctors travel with the army, providing medical care for wounded soldiers and to Salvadoran peasants as part of the army's civic action program. A Salvadoran Air Force colonel told one RRII doctor: "Because you come down here and we see you again and again getting dirty and bloody, we trust you."

By April 1985 RRII had sent 12 medical teams to Central America. The February 1984 medical team sent to El Salvador performed initial and refresher first-aid training for 18 helicopter doorgunners and presented them with 15 medical kits for use aboard their aircraft. As a funding pitch, RRII states: "For the price of a case of beer you can help save a life and get a blow in at communism at the same time."

Soldier of Fortune (SOF)
Omega Group
Boulder, CO

Principals: Robert K. Brown, Harry Aderholt, Alexander M.S. McColl.

Omega Group is the corporate entity that publishes Soldier of Fortune and two other magazines, Guns & Action and Combat Weapons. Omega Group also operates a mail order weapons business called SOF Exchange. The Omega Group was apparently named in honor of the anti-Castro Cuban exile group, Omega Seven, which was responsible for the 1976 assassination of former Chilean ambassador Orlando Letelier and his colleague Ronni Moffitt. A reporter who infiltrated SOF wrote: "Given the evidence I think a strong case can be made that the SOF group is in fact a paramilitary operation of the CIA (or a faction of that agency) and is engaged in obvious operations for that group."

The Omega Group founded Soldier of Fortune: The Journal of the Professional Adventurer in 1975. The glossy magazine boasts of 200,000 circulation and annual gross revenue of $6.9 million. In the past, SOF depended on Vietnam veterans as its main readership but it now attracts many others including large numbers of high school students, supporters of the New Right, and men infused with the Rambo spirit. It publishes ads for paramilitary operations and several pro-Nazi articles have appeared in the magazine. SOF's promotional slogan is: "Be A Man Among Men."

Published by Robert Brown, SOF carries articles that offer information on how to obtain and use weapons and explosives, how to conduct interrogations, and methods of psychological warfare. It advertises weapons and special gear for military adventurers, and its classified section frequently includes ads offering services of "experienced" mercenaries.

The magazine also regularly publishes articles about SOF's own training and combat missions in Central America. A recent article by contributing editor Peter G. Kokalis, who has been identified as having worked with U.S. Army Intelligence, was headlined: "Atlacatl Assault: SOF in Combat with El Salvador's Elite Battalion." Another SOF issue featured a photo of SOF's Explosives/Demolitions editor John Donovan, who "teaches Salvadorans basic demolitions." In a later issue, Donovan was

pictured with his hand resting on a skull, with a caption that read: "John Donovan and friend (a dead Salvadoran guerrilla)."

The profits of the magazine underwrite military training for several counterrevolutionary efforts, notably support for the Shiite insurgents in Afghanistan and the contras. SOF also promotes anticommunist humanitarianism by advocating that its readers donate funds and supplies to Refugee Relief International, an organization headed by SOF editors.

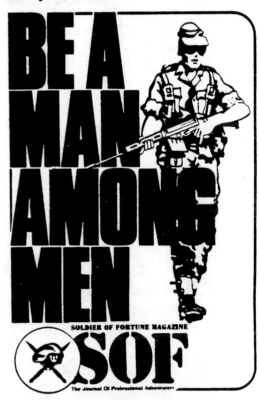

SOF's El Salvador/Nicaragua Defense Fund has sent over 12,000 pounds of new and used military gear (but "no weapons or ammo," says SOF) to the armed forces of El Salvador. SOF acknowledges that some of its shipments to Central America are "piggybacked" aboard U.S. military aircraft. From February 1982 to August 1985 SOF sent over a dozen training teams to El Salvador to "supplement the efforts of the U.S. MilGroup." Training missions teach first aid for Medevac crews, machine-gun marksmanship, sniping, and anti-guerrilla urban warfare.

One such mission provided training for the army's Deep Reconnaissance Platoon, known as the Bush Beasts. SOF trainers, unlike U.S. military advisers, frequently accompany army combat forays. SOF advisers deny taking an active part in the fighting, claiming that they only carry hand guns for their own self-defense. Henry Claflin, the magazine's Central America editor, personally led at least three training missions to El Salvador and Honduras. Before joining SOF, Claflin worked overseas under a private contract for four years as a weapons consultant for AID. Claflin has also been a security consultant for the State Department, helping provide protection for government VIPs traveling abroad. He now owns and operates the Starlight Training Center in Liberal, Missouri, a company that offers courses in outdoor survival, ranger-type operations and parachute operations to carefully-screened clients, many of them from law enforcement and military backgrounds.

SOF has sponsored numerous missions to Honduras to train contras and regularly supplies the Nicaraguan contras with military equipment. In 1985, SOF circulated a Spanish-language poster in Central America that offered a $1 million reward to the first pilot to fly a Soviet attack helicopter out of Nicaragua.

U.S. Council for World Freedom (USCWF)
Phoenix, AZ

Principals: Board of Directors: John Singlaub (president), Daniel Graham (vice chair), W.A. "John" Johnson (treasurer, president of Research Publications), Dr. Anthony Bouscaren (Le Moyne University professor), Walter Chopiwskyj (National Captive Nations Committee), Anna C. Chennault (president of TAC International), Lev E. Dobriansky (Ambassador to Bahamas on leave of absence), John LeBoutillier (former U.S. representative), Anthony Kubek (Troy State University professor), Robert Morris (former chief counsel of Senate Internal Security Subcommittee), J. A. Parker (chair of The Lincoln Institute for Research and Education), Dr. Stefan Possony (professor Emeritus, Hoover Institute), Major General J. Milnor Roberts (ret.) (Committee for a Free Afghanistan), Kathleen Teague Rothschild (American Legislative Exchange Council), Dr. Victor T. H. Tsuan (Fairleigh Dickinson University professor). Advisory Board: Dr. N.M. Camardese (Americanism Foundation), John Fisher (president of American Security Council), Burt Hurlbut (president of First Texas Royalty & Exploration Co.), John S. McCain III (U.S. representative from Arizona), Andy Messing, Howard Phillips (The Conservative Caucus), Eldon Rudd (U.S. representative from Arizona), Fred Schlafly (husband of Phyllis Schlafly, constitutional lawyer), Gerald B. Solomon (U.S. representative from New York).

The United States has had a chapter of the World Anti-Communist League (WACL) since 1969 but the organization has been split a number of times by debate over the presence of neo-Nazis within WACL. During the late 1970s, the election of self-proclaimed white supremacist Dr. Roger Pearson as president of WACL split the U.S. chapter which was then called the American Council for World Freedom.

USCWF began in 1981 under Singlaub's leadership and with international financing from WACL. USCWF has chapters scattered throughout the United States. Bruce Jones, a large U.S. landowner in Costa Rica who has provided logistical support for the contras, recently helped organize USCWF's new Tucson chapter.

USCWF is a major private source of funds and supplies to the contras. The Miami Herald in 1985 estimated that USCWF channels upwards of $500,000 a month to the contras for a total of as much as $10 million in the last couple of years. Contributions come from individuals, community organizations, and corporations.

Singlaub says that nearly half of USCWF donations originate in Texas. Its major contributors include: Joseph Coors, Bert Hurlbut, Howell Instruments, Harry Lucas Jr. (Dallas oilman) Jack Cox (one-time Republican candidate for Governor, co-author with Anastasio Somoza of Nicaragua Betrayed), Ellen Garwood, and Charlie Wilson (Texas state representative).

Singlaub says that money collected in the United States is used to buy only nonlethal supplies, thereby not violating American neutrality and arms export laws. USCWF funds have bought boats and clothing but not weapons for FDN and MISURA, he claims. The retired general says he uses WACL's international contacts to obtain lethal military aid from foreign governments, individuals, and corporations. The New York Times said that USCWF recently provided a short take off and landing aircraft to the contras, supposedly to be used for transporting humanitarian aid. According to Singlaub, Fred Ikle, Under Secretary for Defense Policy, and Nestor Sanchez, Deputy Secretary of Defense for Inter-American Affairs, have helped USCWF by having the organization's supplies placed on U.S. Navy and Air Force craft headed for Central America.

Current USCWF projects include: 1) formation of a coalition of anticommunist groups called the Coalition for World Freedom; 2) "Project Boots" to provide work boots to freedom fighters in Nicaragua and Afghanistan; 3) "Captive Nations Park" to be built in San Antonio as a monument to countries subjugated by communism; 4) pressure to ensure that Peace Corps volunteers are given "anticommunist training" so that "every Peace Corps volunteer will understand thoroughly the strategy, tactics, and methodology of communism;" and 5) support of the contras through the provision of non-lethal equipment like small boats and helicopters and the organization's "Freedom Fighter Friendship Kits."

World Anti-Communist League (WACL)

Principals: John Singlaub (chair), Daniel Graham, Robert Close (Belgium), Ku Cheng Kang (Taiwan), Manuel Frutos (Paraguay), Yaroslav Stetsko (Ukranian).

WACL was founded in 1967 at a conference in Taipei as an outgrowth of the Asian People's Anti-Communist League. It has counted on the close backing of the Taiwan government and has served as an adjunct to the government's foreign service. Its original purpose was to serve as an "anti-communist united front" to support "materially and spiritually" the worldwide struggle against Soviet and Chinese imperialism." Its founders included the supporters of Reverend Sun Myung Moon, whose aide Osami Kuboki controls WACL's chapter in Japan. Besides Taiwan, WACL has received steady support from the governments of South Korea, Saudi Arabia, and Paraguay. It currently has chapters in over 50 countries.

Anticommunism and antisemitism have been the key ideologies of WACL. Executive board member Yaroslav Stetso was a prominent WWII Nazi collaborator who briefly headed a Nazi puppet government in the Ukraine, and Dr. Manuel Frutos, another WACL director, organized the 1979 WACL conference in Paraguay to which he invited several former Nazi SS officers and neo-fascists. Observers called it the "most Nazified" of all WACL annual meetings.

The 1978 chair of WACL, Dr. Roger Pearson, began his career as a racial propagandist during his stay in India as a tea planter. In 1956, he started publishing the racist magazine Northern World. Pearson in 1977 joined the founding editorial board of Policy Review, a quarterly journal published by the Heritage Foundation. He has authored books entitled Eugenics and Race and Blood Groups and Race, and in recent years has received at least $36,000 from the Pioneer Fund (a foundation dedicated to scientific racism and run by political associates of Senator Jesse Helms). In 1982, President Reagan wrote a letter to Pearson, thanking him for his "substantial contributions to promoting and upholding those ideals and principles we value at home and abroad."

WACL has used its anti-Semitic credentials to solicit money from wealthy Arabs. In a 1981 report, the Anti-Defamation League of B'nai B'rith described WACL as "a gathering place for extremists, racists and anti-Semites."

WACL is also closely linked with Latin American death squads and right wing extremists. The Somoza family were WACL members for many years. WACL's Latin American chapter, the Latin America Anti-Communist Confederation (CAL), was directed by a secret order of Nazi sympathizers called Los Tecos based in Guadalajara, Mexico. The secret society grew out of a right-wing counterrevolutionary movement known as Los Cristeros during the Mexican revolution early in this century.

Mario Sandoval Alarcon, the long-time WACL representative in Guatemala, created the extremist National Liberation Movement (NLM), which organized the White Hand death squads in Guatemala in the 1960s. In the 1970s, Sandoval introduced Roberto D'Aubuisson, a right-wing Salvadoran leader, to his WACL contacts in Argentina, who later came to El Salvador to set up safe houses for the newly established Salvadoran death squads and instruct the security forces in the techniques of countersubversion. "Our movements are all coordinated out of Mexico City," said a leader of a Honduran death squad. "The name of the front group there is CAL," which he also referred to as the White Hand.

Internal objections to the antisemitism of WACL leadership began to surface in the early 1970s. In 1974, the principal U.S. constituent member of WACL, the American Council for World Freedom, pulled out of the organization in protest. The Council on American Affairs, an organization controlled by Roger Pearson, became the official U.S. affiliate. The Rev. Sun Myung Moon's political organization, the Freedom

Leadership Foundation, applauded the pullout by the American Council as a "repudiation of fascism." Since the 1970s CAUSA has been part of WACL through the Japanese chapter.

Singlaub claims that WACL has since been purged of its Nazis and death squad members. He cites the recent expulsion of the Mexican chapter and the reorganization of CAL into a new Latin wing called Federacion de Entidades Democraticas de America Latina (FEDAL). But observers criticize these changes as being largely cosmetic. Former WACL member Geoffrey Stewart-Smith says that the difference between CAL and FEDAL is "merely a name change." In 1985, Mario Sandoval Alcaron appeared as usual at the annual WACL convention in Dallas, and Singlaub said he assumed that the Latin American chapter had cleared Sandoval to attend.

Little really had changed in WACL when Singlaub took over the chair of WACL in 1984. It was still an organization built on a united front among fascists and anticommunists. Singlaub has not promised to clean house but he did promise to make WACL an "action agency" that did more than wring their hands over the communist threat. In the last two years, WACL, under Singlaub's stewardship, has emerged from the obscurity of the lunatic fringe of the right wing to win new respectability and power. President Reagan has even sent his personal greetings to recent WACL conventions. Under Reagan, WACL members have been appointed to ambassadorships in the Bahamas, Costa Rica, and Guatemala. At the 1985 conference, Singlaub read the following from President Reagan extending his "warm greetings," saying: "Our combined efforts are moving the tide of history toward world freedom. I send you all who help in the crusade for liberty my best wishes." It is indeed a combined effort. Years before President Reagan began calling anticommunist insurgents "freedom fighters," WACL was using the term; and WACL, long before the surfacing of the Reagan Doctrine, had advocated direct aid to guerrilla groups fighting leftist governments.

WACL's international network has been a key element in the campaign to raise funds to support the contras. "I can go to any country in the world and I know that I have a friend there who can help me get in touch with people I need," said Singlaub. Major U.S. contributors to WACL include: Bert Hurlbut, Wendell Hobbs (McAllen, Texas), Edward J. Drake, (corporate attorney and member of CNP), the Hunt brothers, Tarlton "Topsy" King (Corpus Christi oil fortune heiress), Scott Parrott (Parrott Oil Corp, Dallas). As part of its 1985 convention in Dallas, WACL hosted a "Freedom Fighters' Dinner" to honor leaders of eight anticommunist rebel groups.

World Medical Relief (WMR)
Detroit, MI

Principals: Irene M. Auberlin.

WMR's slogan, "dedicated to the service of God's poor," hides its function as a front for CIA and counterinsurgency operations. Irene Auberlin and her late husband, Lester, founded WMR in 1953 after watching a television program about a Korean orphan named "Little Georgie Ascom." They established the organization to collect supplies for Korean war victims and soon the Auberlins were overseeing an international relief network.

In the mid-1950s, WMR became the main supplier of Dr. Tom Dooley's medical clinic five miles from the Chinese border. Dooley worked closely with the CIA, AID, Air America Airlines (a CIA airline), and the Pentagon. (See Tom Dooley Foundation/InterMed). In 1964, WMR began working with the Colonel Harry Aderholt and the Air Commandos. Its donations were transferred by Aderholt to CIA employee Edgar "Pop" Buell, who supplied the secret 30,000-man Meo army. Buell was posing as an official of the Agency for International Development (AID). During the Vietnam war, the Air Commandos stationed Hap Lutz (a current director of the Air Commandos Association) at the Selfridge Air Force Base near Michigan to better coordinate supplies from WMR. Supplies also went directly into Vietnam to back the U.S. pacification campaign admin-

istered by Robert Komer, a long-time friend of WMR board member Kensinger Jones.

For over two decades, WMR has maintained its links with Aderholt and the Air Commandos. A plaque hanging in Auberlin's office gives tribute to this connection. The plaque signed by Aderholt reads: "To Irene M. Auberlin...In grateful recognition of your outstanding contribution to the advancement of the special air warfare mission..."

In an investigative report on WMR, writer Russ Bellant said that Aderholt is probably "the most active liaison between WMR and U.S. covert operations in Central America." In the mid-1960s, WMR, upon the urging of Aderholt, began supplying military civic action programs in Central America. In 1972, the U.S. Southern Command (SOUTHCOM) in its newspaper reported that WMR's "distribution in Latin America is handled primarily by U.S. Southern Command, as part of its extensive medical civic action program throughout the area."

WMR still sends supplies to Southeast Asia but its main focus today is Central America. It is a principal supplier of the humanitarian work of such groups as the Air Commandos, Refugee Relief International, Christian Broadcasting Network, and National Defense Council in Guatemala, Honduras, Costa Rica, and El Salvador.

The WMR executive committee and board of directors include representatives of Kresge, General America Life Insurance Co., Manufacturers Bank, Detroit Edison Co., Ford Motor Co., General Motors, Chrysler, Michigan Consolidated Gas, and Bell Telephone.

Air Commando Association

ACA Newsletter, August 1984; Phone interview by
Deb Preusch with Charles Hicks, February 11,
1986; Synapses, "The Christian Broadcasting
Network: Unholy Alliances," no date; Phone interview by Deb Preusch with Harry Aderholt, January
1986; The Nation, November 2, 1985; ACA Newsletter, May 1985; ACA Newsletter, September 1984.

American Foundation for Resistance International

Encyclopedia of Associations, 1986.

American Freedom Fighters Association

Common Cause Magazine, September/October 1985.

Americares

Washington Post, December 27, 1984; "Americares
Fact Sheet", June 1985; Links, Central America
Health Rights Network, Vol.2, Nos.1 & 2, 1985;
Correspondence with Americares, July 26, 1985.

Brigade 2506

Encyclopedia of Associations, 1986; Counterspy,
March-May, 1984; Latin American Index, September
1, 1985; Financial Times, October 11, 1985;
Common Cause Magazine, September/October 1985.

Caribbean Commission

Wall Street Journal, June 14, 1985; Wall Street
Journal, September 14, 1984; Lance Hill, "Ex-Klan
Leader Joins Contras," Second Line, Vol. 1, No.
4; Phone interview by Deb Preusch with Lance
Hill, April 15, 1986.

Christian Broadcasting Network

Synapses, "The Christian Broadcasting Network:
Unholy Alliances" no date; Interview by Deb
Preusch with CBN, July 22, 1985; Newsweek October
14, 1985; Chicago Tribune, June 26, 1985; Wall
Street Journal, October 17, 1985; Synapses press
release April 13, 1985; Miami Herald, June 14,
1985; Sojourners, October 1985; Synapses press
release June 27, 1985; The Virginian-Pilot July
11, 1985; Washington Post, November 2, 1985; New
York Times, July 15, 1984; Miami Herald, September 9, 1984; Wall Street Journal, September 14,
1984; Newsweek, October 14, 1985; Chicago Tribune,
June 6, 1985; Christian Century, March 5, 1986.

Citizens for America

NBC News May 21, 1985; Al Weinrub, "Coors Brews
More Than Beer," Labor Report on Central America,
September/October, 1985.

Civilian Materiel Assistance

Time, September 17, 1984; Time, May 27, 1985;
Nation, March 9, 1985; The Guardian, December 25,
1985; "Pacific News Service", May 24, 1984;
Covert Action Information Bulletin, Fall 1984;
The Texas Observer, March 7, 1986; New York
Times, September 10, 1984; Dallas Life Magazine,
February 9, 1986; Wall Street Journal, June 14,
1985; CMA information brochure, no date; Miami
Herald, January 21, 1985; Houston Post, April 14,
1985; New York Times, April 19, 1985; New York
Times, July 8, 1986; New York Times, July 11, 1986

Coalition for World Freedom

The Texas Observer, March 7, 1986; WACL Press
Conference with General Singlaub, July 1985.

Concerned Citizens for Democracy

Miami Herald, June 27, 1985.

CAUSA

Washington Post, May 3, 1985; Washington Post,
September 17, 1984; Washington Post, August 28,
1983; News Notes, Maryknoll Justice and Peace
Office, January 1986; Washington Post, September
16, 1984; Covert Action Information Bulletin,
Fall 1984.

Council for National Policy

The Texas Observer, March 7, 1986; CNP letterhead and Officers List; Miami Herald, January 21,
1985; The Guardian, February 19, 1986; Cindy Buhl
"Covert War: Private Aid to the Contras", no
date.

Democracy International

The Guardian, June 26, 1985.

Tom Dooley Foundation/InterMed USA

Metro Times, October 9-15, 1985; Synapses, "The
Christian Broadcasting Network: Unholy Alliances," no date.

Eagle Forum

Dallas Life Magazine, February 9, 1986; Christian Science Monitor, December 10, 1985.

Family Foundation of America

Interview by Deb Preusch with Kenneth Wells, November 1985; The News and Observer, November 20, 1985.

Freedom's Friends

The Texas Observer, March 7, 1986.

Friends of the Americas

"FOA Fact Sheet", January 1986; Wall Street Journal, June 14, 1985; New York Times, July 15, 1984; The Nation, October 6, 1984; Interview by Deb Preusch with Carmen Winkler, December 1985.

Gulf and Caribbean

The Texas Observer, March 7, 1986.

Institute for Regional and International Studies

Boston Globe, December 30, 1984; Village Voice, October 1, 1985.

International Aid

Air Commando Newsletter, February, 1985; Synapses, "The Christian Broadcasting Network: Unholy Alliances," no date.

International Relief Friendship Foundation

Arms Control and Foreign Policy Caucus, "Who are the Contras?" April 23, 1985; Washington Post, September 17, 1984.

Knights of Malta

Correspondence with Gerard T. Coughlin, Asociacion de El Salvador de la Soberana Orden Militar y Hospitalaria de Malta, March 5, 1986; Washington Post, December 27, 1984, Mother Jones, July 1983; National Catholic Reporter, October 11, 1983.

National Defense Council Foundation

Village Voice, November 26, 1985; The Nation, November 2, 1985; The Texas Observer, March 7, 1986; ACA Newsletter, February 1985; Miami Herald, December 17, 1984.

National Endowment for the Preservation of Liberty

The Texas Observer, March 7, 1986; In These Times, April 16, 1986; New York City Tribune, March 16, 1986.

Nicaragua Development Council

Sojourners, October 1985; FDN Bulletin, November 1, 1985.

Nicaraguan Freedom Fund

Los Angeles Times, June 11, 1985; Washington Post, May 7, 1985; Washington Post, May 9, 1985.

Nicaraguan Patriotic Association

Sojourners, October 1985; The Texas Observer, March 7, 1986.

Nicaragua Refugee Fund

Washington Post, September 3, 1985; Information from NRF.

Pro-America Educational Foundation

New York Times, July 15, 1984; Arms Control and Foreign Policy Caucus, "Who Are the Contras?" April 23, 1985.

PRODEMCA

Washington Post, March 19, 1986; Washington Post, March 21, 1986.

Refugee Relief International Inc.

Soldier of Fortune, August, 1984; Common Cause Magazine, September/October 1985; Washington Times, April 26, 1985.

Soldier of Fortune

New York Times, September 23, 1985; New York Times, July 15, 1984; Soldier of Fortune, August 1985; Dirty Work: The CIA in Africa Edited by Ellen Ray, William Schaap, Karl Van Meter and Louis Wolf, (Lyly Stuart Inc, Secacucs NJ, 1978);

Soldier of Fortune, April 1985; Wall Street Journal, September 6, 1984; Miami Herald, September 9, 1984.

U.S. Council for World Freedom

Information sent from USCWF; New Republic, September 30, 1985; New York Times, August 27, 1985; The Texas Observer, March 7, 1986; Washington Post, May 3, 1985; New York Times, September 15, 1985; Christian Science Monitor, August 22, 1985; Miami Herald, January 21, 1985; "Private Funding of the Contra," Witness for Peace and Coalition for Nicaragua, August 1985; From "USCWF: Goals and Objectives," no date; Common Cause Magazine, September/October 1985.

World Anti-Communist League

Village Voice, October 22, 1985; Dallas Life Magazine, February 9, 1986; New York Times, August 10, 1985; New York Times, August 27, 1985; New Republic, September 30, 1985; Washington Post, Jack Anderson, September 11, 1984; Washington Post, Jack Anderson, January 30, 1984; Washington Post, Jack Anderson, February 9, 1984; The Guardian, October 2, 1985; Los Angeles Times, September 16, 1985; Village Voice, May 7, 1985.

World Medical Relief

WMR Newsletter, Vol. 1 Issue 11; The Metro Times, October 9-15, 1985; The Nation, November 2, 1985; ACA Newsletter, February 1985; Soldier of Fortune, August 1984.

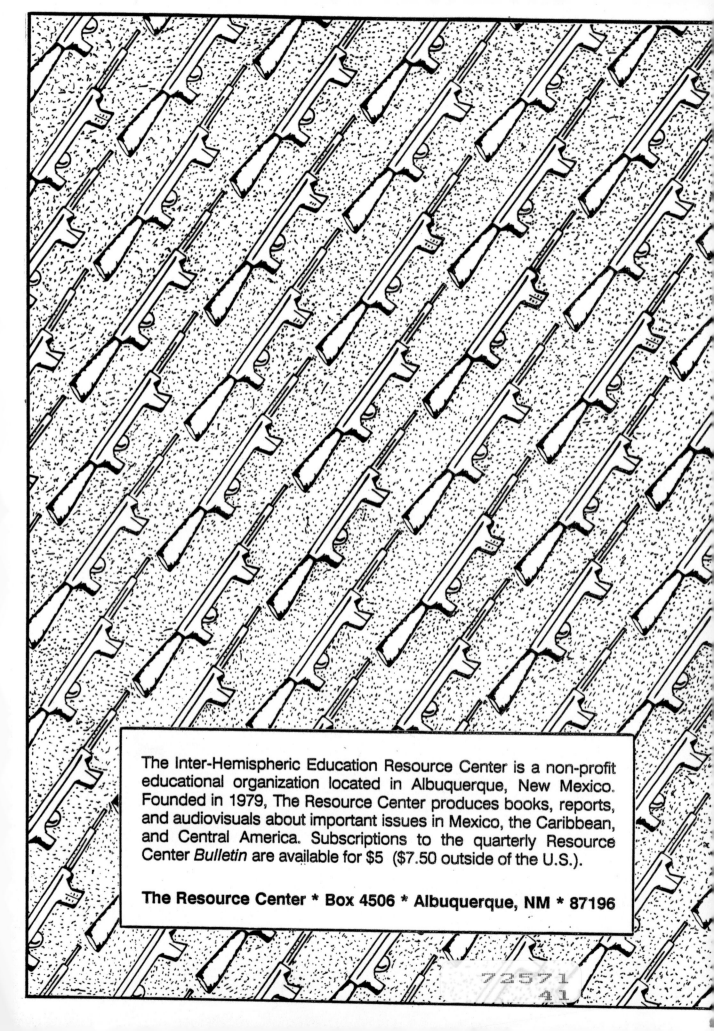

The Inter-Hemispheric Education Resource Center is a non-profit educational organization located in Albuquerque, New Mexico. Founded in 1979, The Resource Center produces books, reports, and audiovisuals about important issues in Mexico, the Caribbean, and Central America. Subscriptions to the quarterly Resource Center *Bulletin* are available for $5 ($7.50 outside of the U.S.).

The Resource Center * Box 4506 * Albuquerque, NM * 87196